FIFTY YEARS IN THE KAREN REVOLUTION IN BURMA

FIFTY YEARS IN THE KAREN REVOLUTION IN BURMA

The Soldier and the Teacher

Saw Ralph and Naw Sheera

Edited by Stephanie Olinga-Shannon

With an introduction by Martin Smith

SOUTHEAST ASIA PROGRAM PUBLICATIONS

AN IMPRINT OF CORNELL UNIVERSITY PRESS   ITHACA AND LONDON

First published 2019 by Cornell University Press

Library of Congress Cataloging-in-Publication Data

Names: Ralph, Saw, 1930– author. | Sheera, Naw, 1932– author. | Olinga-Shannon,
    Stephanie, editor.
Title: Fifty years in the Karen revolution in Burma : the soldier and the teacher / Saw
    Ralph and Naw Sheera ; edited by Stephanie Olinga-Shannon ; with an introduction
    by Martin Smith.
Other titles: 50 years in the Karen revolution in Burma
Description: First edition. | Ithaca : Southeast Asia Program Publications, an
    imprint of Cornell University Press, 2020. | Includes bibliographical references
    and index.
Identifiers: LCCN 2019018733 (print) | LCCN 2019019512 (ebook) | ISBN
    9781501746949 (pbk.)
Subjects: LCSH: Ralph, Saw, 1930– | Sheera, Naw, 1932– | Karen (Southeast Asian
    people)—Burma—Biography. | Karen State (Burma)—History—Autonomy
    and independence movements. | Insurgency—Burma—Karen State. | Burma—
    Politics and government—1948– | Karen National Liberation Army. | Karen
    Women's Organization.
Classification: LCC DS528.2.K35 R35 2020 (print) | LCC DS528.2.K35 (ebook) |
    DDC 959.105—dc23
LC record available at https://lccn.loc.gov/2019018733
LC ebook record available at https://lccn.loc.gov/2019019512

ISBN 978-1-5017-4696-3 (epub/mobi ebook)
ISBN 978-1-5017-4695-6 (pdf ebook)

To the Karen people

Contents

Editor's Preface

This book comprises two very different, almost opposite, perspectives on five decades in the world's longest civil war. Here the same conflict—the beginnings, daily life, struggles, and joys—is explored through two lenses: that of a soldier and that of a teacher.

Brigadier Saw Ralph Hodgson and Naw Sheera Hodgson's enduring involvement in the Karen Revolution has afforded them a long and broad view of the conflict.[1] From day one in 1949 through to their retirement in 1997, they were drawn into some of the key events of the revolution and actively worked with some of its key players.

Saw Ralph's story is that of a combatant, a guerrilla, a general, and a strategist. He came from a privileged cosmopolitan Anglo-Karen family but chose to walk away from that to live as a revolutionary in the jungle. He found success in the rebel army and rose quickly through the ranks. He became general staff officer for the Karen National Liberation Army (KNLA) and took part in some of its most definitive events. In the KNLA he found what he loved: adventure, camaraderie, a sense of purpose, and a life very different from what was expected of him. But it wasn't without great sacrifice. He was forced to cut all contact with his close-knit family, and he expected never to see them again. Drawn to the excitement of battle, Saw Ralph was forever away from his wife, Naw Sheera, and their children.

Naw Sheera was born in the jungle. The civil war was thrust on her remote village when the Burmese burned it to the ground and she made a remarkable escape. At a young age she learned to survive and depended on these skills to raise four children alone in the midst of the revolution. As a young woman she was determined to become a teacher. That determination remains today in her encouragement of her grandchildren's education and spiritual growth. Her Christian faith is her unshakeable rock, and by her own recognition it was through faith and prayer that she survived.

---

1. "Saw" is a Karen honorific equivalent to "Mr." in English, while "Naw" is an honorific for Karen adult women equivalent to "Mrs." or "Ms." Both honorifics are primarily used by Sgaw Karens, one of the Karen subgroups. To protect his family, Saw Ralph never used his family name after he joined the revolution. He was known only as "Saw Ralph" or by his rank—for example, "Colonel Ralph".

Married for over fifty years, Saw Ralph and Naw Sheera have intertwined lives, but their journeys didn't truly intersect until they reached old age, after they had left the war behind and moved to a life of peace in suburban Australia.

When the Hodgsons arrived in Australia, Saw Ralph's relatives came from all over the world to see him. They wanted to know where he'd been and what he'd done during the fifty years he was away. Ever a practical man, Saw Ralph decided to write down his story so he didn't have to explain it over and over again. He learned to use a computer and began writing the details. Some years later his niece Maureen arranged for me to help pull it all together. As we heard more of the incredible life Naw Sheera had lived we felt we would be remiss not to include her story in the book too.

We started with Saw Ralph. Sitting in their living room in Perth, he told me the stories of his adventures. Despite being in his late eighties, his memory was incredible. He could remember precise guns used in particular battles, but it soon became clear that it was harder for him to articulate his feelings and reactions. He was forced to explore key events in his life that he had not contemplated since they happened. He had to face his drinking problem and the dark days in the KNLA's history. At first, Saw Ralph refused to include any reference to religion even though his Christian faith has played a pervasive role in his life. He was burned by his experience with the Buddhist split from the KNLA. Always the loyal soldier, he was hesitant to discuss events that reflected poorly on the KNLA. After frank discussions on the importance of writing a warts-and-all account he agreed to include the events.

Likewise, Naw Sheera struggled to express how she felt. At first, she would not discuss her many brothers who died in infancy and her own son's early death. It became clear that this would be a difficult emotional journey for them both. What started as a military memoir became a deeply personal story in which their strengths and flaws were laid bare. Over time they learned how to describe their feelings and open up to each other—and to me—about experiences they had suppressed for decades.

Over the four years it took to compile this book, I got to know Naw Sheera, Saw Ralph, and their family well, and they got to know mine. I attended many prayer services to celebrate birthdays and anniversaries. I watched as Saw Ralph made speeches on Hero's Day just as I imagine he had done when addressing his troops in the jungle.

There were practical challenges too. Saw Ralph's English is excellent, if a little old fashioned, so we were able to communicate directly. Naw Sheera speaks four languages, none of which I understand, unfortunately. So a grandchild of one of Naw Sheera's friends translated for her. Both Saw Ralph and Naw Sheera struggled with dates and the sequence of events. Over such long lifetimes, precise dates had lost their relevance. Furthermore, all of Saw Ralph's personal documents were left behind at the KNLA headquarters in Manerplaw when it was destroyed by the Burmese armed forces, so we fact checked where possible and resequenced where necessary.

Saw Ralph once showed me a certificate he had received from the Australian Karen Association and told me, "After fifty years in the Karen Revolution this is all I have." There is still no victory, no independent Kawthoolei for the Karen people. For Saw Ralph and Naw Sheera, I think this book is also about having something to show for the decades of struggle. Here they share what they did, their resilience, how they succeeded, and how they survived.[2]

We wish to thank Jangai Jap, a PhD candidate in political science at George Washington University for her assistance with background research; Xiaoxue Xiao, a graduate of Renmin University of China and of the Master of Architecture program at Columbia University's Graduate School of Architecture, Planning, and Preservation, for her assistance in preparing the images and maps; and Elizabeth Sein, granddaughter of a Karen official, who generously contributed her services as a translator in Perth. We would also like to thank the editorial team at Cornell University Press and the two anonymous reviewers for their helpful comments on earlier drafts.

---

2. In 1989, following mass demonstrations for democracy that were brutally repressed, the ruling military junta Burmanized place names in Myanmar. The name of the country was changed from "Burma" to "Myanmar," and "Rangoon" became known as "Yangon." The names are interchangeable in the Burmese language, but their use has become a politicized issue. "Myanmar" is the main term in the country and for official purposes, but "Burma" is still often used in historical writings and the English language. Saw Ralph and Naw Sheera, like many Karens, continue to use pre-1989 place names, including "Burma" for the country and "Rangoon" for its largest city. They were at war with the Burmese military in 1989 and the move represented a further "Burmanization" of the country by the ethnic-Burman military. Additionally, most of the events discussed in this book occurred before place names were Burmanized in 1989. Therefore, the pre-1989 official place names are used throughout this book. "Burman" (Bamar) generally refers to the majority ethnic group, while "Burmese" is used for all peoples in the country at large.

Abbreviations

ABSDF	All Burma Students Democratic Front
AFO	Anti-Fascist Organization
AFPFL	Anti-Fascist People's Freedom League
BDA	Burma Defence Army
BIA	Burma Independence Army
BNA	Burma National Army
CPB	Communist Party of Burma
DAB	Democratic Alliance of Burma
DKBA	Democratic Karen Buddhist Army
KNA	Karen National Association
KNDO	Karen National Defence Organization
KNLA	Karen National Liberation Army
KNU	Karen National Union
KNUP	Karen National United Party
KWO	Karen Women's Organization
NDF	National Democratic Front
NLD	National League for Democracy
NMSP	New Mon State Party
NULF	National United Liberation Front
SLORC	State Law and Order Restoration Council
SPDC	State Peace and Development Council
UMP	Union Military Police
UNHCR	United Nations High Commissioner for Refugees

Timeline of Key Events

1930   Ralph Ernest Hodgson is born

1932   Sheera Ba Tin is born

1942   The Japanese invade Burma

1945   The Japanese leave Burma and the British return

1947   The Karen National Union (KNU) is established

1948   Burma gains independence from the British

1949   The Karen Revolution begins and Ralph joins

1950   KNU leader Saw Ba U Gyi is assassinated

1953   The Karen National United Party (KNUP) is formed

1955   Sheera becomes a missionary teacher

1961   Ralph and Sheera marry

1962   General Ne Win seizes power in a coup d'état
        Ne Win's Burmese Way to Socialism is imposed

1963   Dey Law Hodgson is born and dies

1965   Ler Paw (John) Hodgson is born

1968   Ler Gay (James) Hodgson is born

1970   Ralph is posted to Karen National Liberation Army (KNLA) headquarters at Manerplaw
        The family moves to nearby Kler Thay Lu village
        KNU forms the National United Liberation Front (NULF) with ex-PM U Nu

1971   Mina Hodgson is born

1973   Paw Nay Thah (Judith) Hodgson is born

1976   Bo Mya becomes KNU president and the KNUP is dissolved
        KNU coestablishes the ethnic National Democratic Front with nine different ethnic political parties and organizations.

1985   Sheera joins the Karen Women's Organization (KWO)

1988   Prodemocracy protests take place across Burma
        The State Law and Order Restoration Council (SLORC) assumes power
        KNU joins the Democratic Alliance of Burma (DAB) with prodemocracy exiles

1990   The National League for Democracy (NLD) wins the general election by a landslide
        The National Coalition Government of the Union of Burma (NCGUB) is established at Manerplaw (as a government in exile)

1992   The National Council of the Union of Burma (NCUB) is formed in KNU
        headquarters with NLD MPs-elect
1994   The Democratic Karen Buddhist Army (DKBA) is formed, splits from KNU
1995   The Burma Army captures KNU headquarters in Manerplaw; Sheera flees
        to Thailand
1997   Sheera retires from the Karen Women's Organization
        Ralph is granted long leave from the KNLA
        Ralph and Sheera move to a refugee camp in Bangkok
        SLORC is renamed the State Peace and Development Council (SPDC)
2001   Ralph and Sheera move to Perth, Australia
2007   The Saffron Revolution of Buddhist monks takes place
2008   Cyclone Nargis hits Burma
        The military pushes through its constitution with a 25 percent vote
        ensured in the new parliament
2009   The majority of DKBA is transformed into Border Guard Forces
2011   SPDC steps down and President Thein Sein assumes office. The ceasefire
        between the Myanmar military and the Kachin Independence Organiza-
        tion (KIO) breaks down and conflict resumes.
2012   KNU agrees to an initial ceasefire with the government
2015   KNU signs a Nationwide Ceasefire Agreement with the government
        NLD wins the general election
2016   NLD assumes titular power over the civilian government
        KNU joins the 21st Century Panglong Conference with the government
2017   The peace and reform impasse continues with renewed conflict in Kachin,
        Shan and Rakhine States
        The brutal crackdown on Rohingya spurs flight of 700,000+ refugees
        into Bangladesh
2018   The third meeting of the 21st Century Panglong Conference takes place,
        with still no breakthrough
        A UN report calls for Burmese military leaders to be investigated for
        genocide, crimes against humanity, and war crimes

FIFTY YEARS IN THE KAREN REVOLUTION IN BURMA

INTRODUCTION

Martin Smith

Until a 2012 ceasefire with the government, the armed struggle by the Karen National Union (KNU) was among the longest-running conflicts in the world. From the outbreak of fighting in January 1949, the KNU's history reflects a time of turbulence and state failure in Burma (modern-day Myanmar) that has continued until the present day. Even in 2019, after seven years of KNU ceasefire, ethnic peace remains uncertain and political solutions have not been achieved.

The consequences have been profound. No reliable figures exist for the humanitarian toll. But it is generally accepted that over one million lives have been lost in the political and ethnic violence that spread across the country after independence in 1948. In the process, countless families have been displaced from their homes, national politics have become deeply militarized, and the economy has declined, becoming one of the poorest in Asia.

Despite the long years of conflict, reports or details of the people who have lived through these experiences on the front line remain very scant. In recent years, as the door to the country has opened, there has been greater international recognition of the deep traumas that many communities have passed through. There is also a greater effort among the opposing parties themselves to try and achieve national peace and reconciliation. There remains, however, a long way to go. Burma is still at the beginning of transition from decades of ethnic conflict and military rule—not at the end.

Retired brigadier general Saw Ralph and Naw Sheera are not widely known figures in Burma. But, in many ways, their experiences typify the determination with which the foot soldiers of a cause are willing to sacrifice their lives for what they regard as a greater calling. Adding poignancy to their tale is the matter-of-fact manner by which they tell stories of great resonance in what fellow Karens call the "father-to-son war." As Saw Ralph comments: "Modesty and humility are important in Karen culture." But such understatement and avoidance of self-promotion is one of the main reasons why the Karen cause remains so little known in the world outside.

This book helps to fill some of these gaps.[1] During a critical time of national change, Saw Ralph and Naw Sheera were witnesses to many of the key moments in Burma's modern history, from the Second World War and the Battle of Insein to the evolution of the KNU and arrival of the "88 generation" students to take up arms in KNU territory.[2] Saw Ralph's perspective is very much that of a soldier whose duty is always in the front line. Naw Sheera's is that of a woman—very often the most overlooked victims in war—who became a key actor in the development of the Karen Women's Organization while somehow maintaining family life in the conflict zones.

These, however, are only their public personas in the KNU administration. Behind the scenes are stories of real drama that began when fighting broke out during the Japanese occupation in the early 1940s and never truly ended for either of them until they were granted refugee status in Australia over half a

---

1. With the doors to the country largely closed beginning in the mid-twentieth century, book studies on the Karens are limited: they include works by such writers as Donald Smeaton (1887) and Harry Marshall (1922) for the colonial era, Dr. San C. Po (1928) for the growth of Karen nationalism, Ian Morrison (1947) for the events of the Second World War, and Smith Dun (1980) for the memoir of a leading Karen in the transition to Burma's independence. Subsequently, studies on the Karen peoples more often occurred in neighboring Thailand, such as the work of the anthropologist Charles Keyes (1979). One exception was F. K. (Kris) Lehman (1967), who conducted research on the Karenni, who are Karen-related peoples living on the Karen-Shan-Thai borders in the present-day Kayah State. In the early 1990s, I published a history of the Karens, ethnic politics, and conflict in Burma more generally (Smith, 1991, updated 1999), and Jonathan Falla (1991) wrote an eyewitness study of a KNU-controlled territory in the Thai borderlands. Human rights and humanitarian aspects of the Karen conflict have since continued to be followed by such organizations as Amnesty International (e.g., 1999), Burmese Border Consortium (e.g., 2004), and the Karen Human Rights Group (e.g., 2008). Other book accounts of the Karen struggle in the field, largely from the perspective of the Thai border, include those by Benedict Rogers (2004) and Zoya Phan (2009), daughter of the late KNU general-secretary Padoh Mahn Sha La Phan. Meanwhile the Karen political scientist Ardeth Thawnghmung (e.g., 2012) has published studies on the broader aspects of Karen politics and society. Andrew Selth (e.g., 2002) and Mary Callahan (e.g., 2003) have also published studies on the role of the Tatmadaw, long the KNU's principal opponent in the field, and there has been a general increase in academic research on Karen-related issues in recent years, including Mikael Gravers (e.g. 2015 and 2018) and Ashley South (e.g. 2011). But, in general, Karen studies, like many other critical subjects in the country, are still often lacking.

2. The "88 generation" students is the term used to refer to the young people who led pro-democracy protests during the summer of 1988 that led to the downfall of the military socialist government of General Ne Win.

century later. By then, both were well into their sixties. Now, in retirement, they face the challenge of piecing together their lives again, after the loss of so many loved ones and friends, the constant displacement and travels, the unrelieved backdrop of insecurity and threat, and the frequent absences—often of many years' duration—from one another and their families.

The wonder is that they both survived. In the case of Naw Sheera, her Christian faith was a constant support. For Saw Ralph, alcohol was all too often a close companion. But, like all revolutionaries, both Naw Sheera and Saw Ralph also demonstrate a dedication to their cause that shows little sign of wavering. Recalling the 1949 retreat from the Insein battle, Saw Ralph only comments: "Whether the weather was wet or fine, we were still happy, with a high morale and a belief that we were fighting for the rights of our people and for freedom and justice."

Military analysts would argue that that the KNU has been in retreat ever since. But the stoicism of its members helps explain why, seven decades later, the KNU still has not been defeated. Despite reduced territories, KNU die-hards never appear to have been fazed by the military odds. Rather, from Saw Ralph and Naw Sheera's perspective, it was a Buddhist-Christian split in the mid-1990s that constituted the KNU's greatest failure, an internal crisis that allowed a critical advantage to the national armed forces (known as the Tatmadaw) and precipitated the refugee flight of the couple into Thailand.

Established in February 1947, the KNU has witnessed four very different eras of government: parliamentary democracy (1948–62); military socialism (1962–88); military dictatorship (1988–2011); and quasi-civilian democracy (2011–present). Throughout this time, a fundamental principle has been that of the late KNU leader Saw Ba U Gyi: "For us, surrender is out of the question." But beneath this commitment, the KNU has undergone a long ideological journey, reflecting the shifting landscape in postcolonial politics after the Second World War.

At the KNU's 1947 inception, the goal of a Karen Free State, known as Kawthoolei, was a popular dream, bringing the different Karen-related peoples, including Karenni and Pa-O, together in one territory or federation in southeast Burma. But with the Karen population largely separated between two different territories—the rugged borderlands with Thailand in the east and the Irrawaddy Delta region to the west—this goal ultimately proved elusive.[3] Instead, following

---

3. Initially, there were hopes of creating a "pan-Karen" movement among all Karen-related peoples. But since independence, four nationality movements have evolved: the mainstream Karen (predominantly Pwo and Sgaw), the smaller "Karenni" (i.e., "Red Karen": Kayah, Kayaw and related sub-groups in the modern-day Kayah State), the Kayan, and the Pa-O. For a recent analysis of the Karenni struggle and interrelations with the Karen and other political movements, see Kramer, Russell, and Smith 2018. There is also a historic Karen population in Thailand, but they have never

the loss of Insein, KNU leaders regrouped in the rural countryside to continue the struggle for Karen rights and autonomy. In 1952, the government of Prime Minister U Nu demarcated a Karen State in the rugged borderlands around Hpa'An. But, including less than a quarter of the Karen population in Burma, this remote backwater never satisfied KNU political demands.

In the following years, the KNU was gradually pushed back from urban areas, but battlefield retreat did not disrupt its ability to continue armed struggle. The KNU was far from alone in its resistance to the new government. As central control broke down following the British departure, a diverse array of opposition groups took up arms across the country, including Karenni, Mon, Pa-O, and Rakhine forces in the ethnic borderlands, the Communist Party of Burma (CPB) and Tatmadaw mutineers in central Burma, and Kuomintang remnants who invaded Shan State after Chairman Mao Zedong's victory in China. Against this backdrop, peace talks between the government and the KNU were rare (only in 1949 and 1960). Indeed, one of the greatest challenges for the KNU was its relationship not with the central government but rather with other conflict actors in the field. Such complexity still exists today.

In 1953, in a bid to boost popular support, KNU leaders in the Irrawaddy Delta formed a vanguard movement known as the Karen National United Party

---

become involved in the nationalist struggle of the KNU. During the past three decades, Karen numbers in Thailand have increased due to refugee flight and migration from Burma, and there is a growing Karen diaspora abroad, especially in the USA and Australia. In Burma itself, Karen population statistics remain contentious, a situation that has not been helped by the 2014 Population and Housing Census. Though this was the first census to attempt any real detail since the last British census in 1931, the system of methodology and classification was deeply flawed, and the ethnic data has not been published. In the past, Karen nationalists have claimed population figures of up to seven million if all Karen-related peoples are included. In contrast, government estimates have been less than a third of this number. Part of this large difference has been explained by the perception that many Karens who are Buddhists and/or speak Burmese have been counted as "Burmans" in official statistics, a trend that increased during the twentieth century. There are also differences in estimates for Buddhist and Christian figures among the Karen population. Although Christian numbers have steadily increased since the nineteenth century (mostly Baptists but also Catholics, Seventh Day Adventists, and Anglicans), Buddhists remain in the majority, especially among Pwo and Pa-O communities. In general, Christian Karens have been most prominent in the KNU and other political movements since independence but Buddhist Karens have become more active in social and political affairs, especially in Karen State, since the DKBA split in the mid-1990s. Few Karens are considered to be animists today, but millenarianism, involving aspects of both Buddhism and Christianity, has survived in remote areas in the eastern hills, notably in the Telakhon movement (Smith 1999, 426–28). In the late 1990s, the short-lived "God's Army," led by boy twins, also gained international publicity—and some notoriety—after breaking away from the KNU in the Tenasserim Region and launching two attacks in Thailand. In general, Karen politics and society have become more vibrant since the time of Ralph and Sheera's retirement to Australia, a pace of change that has accelerated since the KNU's ceasefire in 2012. But differences still remain in politics and organization, especially between communities in the eastern borderlands and those living around Yangon and the Irrawaddy Delta.

(KNUP) to lead the KNU as a mass organization among the Karen people. Initially, the new movement had some success. But its activities also sowed the seeds for future discord between left-leaning supporters in the Irrawaddy Delta and conservative leaders in the eastern borderlands. Evidence of the depth of this division first came out into the open during 1963–64 when the KNU's then-president, Saw Hunter Thahmwe, made a breakaway ceasefire with the new military government of General Ne Win, who had seized power the previous year. Few KNU troops, however, followed Hunter Thahmwe back home. As a result, there were, in effect, two KNU parties in armed resistance for the next decade: the KNUP in the Irrawaddy Delta and Pegu Yoma highlands, and the mainstream KNU in the borderlands to the east, where militant opposition resumed against the central government after Thahmwe's departure.

If, however, General Ne Win believed that he would end the country's conflicts by seizing power, he was badly mistaken. Far from suppressing opposition, the 1962 coup poured oil on the flames of rebellion. With the imposition of Ne Win's hermetic Burmese Way to Socialism, the economy swiftly declined as Ne Win sought to impose a one-party system on the country. Beginning in the mid-1960s, Tatmadaw operations were stepped up in the rural countryside, including the notorious Four Cuts campaign that saw many communities forcibly relocated from their villages. But such draconian tactics did not work in the country's rugged borderlands, where a diversity of opposition forces controlled extensive territories. Here armed resistance continued to escalate, boosted in 1968 by China's support to the CPB following anti-Chinese violence in Yangon. A year later, the deposed prime minister U Nu arrived on the Thailand border after his release from detention in Yangon to form a National United Liberation Front (NULF) alliance with the KNU. It marked an extraordinary turnabout in political alignments.

With the Cold War at its height, international analysts asked whether Burma would go into the communist or the pro-Western fold. By the mid-1970s, the CPB's advance had been blocked, the NULF was defunct, and U Nu later returned to Yangon under a 1980 amnesty. But, in many respects, the Cold War era under General Ne Win marked a halcyon period for the KNU in the east, where Saw Ralph and Naw Sheera were now based. During 1975–76, the KNUP had collapsed under the weight of Tatmadaw offensives in the Pegu Yoma and delta regions, setting the scene for the KNU's reunification under Gen. Saw Bo Mya, a formidable commander and anticommunist leader in the Papun hills.

Buoyed by the lucrative cross-border trade with Thailand, for a quarter of a century the KNU was able to manage extensive liberated zones in a quasi mini-state of its own that ran down the Thai border during Ne Win's years in government (1962–88). The KNU headquarters at Manerplaw became the hub of military and political activity, and in 1976 the KNU was a founding member of the National Democratic Front (NDF) with eight other ethnic nationality forces.[4] Until this point, the KNU's policy goals had sometimes appeared ambiguous. But in 1983 the NDF agreed on a common goal of a future "federal union," and this has remained the KNU's political objective ever since. KNU activists, however, were never able to reestablish the party back in the Irrawaddy Delta where much of the Karen population lives. This was a strategic weakness that has continued to undermine the party's influence until the present day.

For a brief moment, the KNU's fortunes then appeared to revive again during mass prodemocracy demonstrations that swept the country in 1988. Subsequently, up to ten thousand students and democracy activists fled the towns and cities into KNU and NDF territories after the military State Law and Order Restoration Council (SLORC) assumed power. As during previous times of government change in 1948–50 and 1962–64, the country's future was highly unpredictable. General Ne Win was forced to step down in the face of the protests, in 1989 the CPB collapsed, and in 1990 the newly formed National League for Democracy (NLD) won Burma's first general election in three decades. Citizens throughout the country wondered: could this finally be the moment when peace and reform would be achieved?

As confusion reigned, KNU territories once again became a main base for political activism. In 1988, a Democratic Alliance of Burma (DAB) was established between the KNU, the NDF, and emerging democracy parties among the ethnic Burman majority. Then, in 1992, a National Council of the Union of Burma (NCUB) was formed, after the new military government blocked the result of the 1990 general election and over a dozen NLD MPs-elect fled to Manerplaw. In a symbolic twist, the NLD MPs were led by Dr. Sein Win, cousin of the NLD leader Aung San Suu Kyi who was under house arrest in Yangon (Rangoon). For a brief moment, activists claimed that there were now two capitals in Burma: Yangon and the KNU headquarters at Manerplaw.

From this high point, momentum stalled, and in the following years the country slipped into another period of political impasse and military rule that was to last almost as long as Ne Win's Burmese Way to Socialism. Despite popular support, neither the NLD nor the NCUB allies were able to gain the political initiative. Instead, the KNU soon found itself in a no man's land between war and peace as the SLORC government began offering ceasefires to ethnic opposition forces. The KNU's aging leaders were uncertain which way to turn. Should they follow other ethnic forces such as the Kachin Independence Organization and New Mon State

---

4. The NDF subsequently became the most significant front in ethnic armed politics after independence. The founding members were the Arakan Liberation Party, the Kachin Independence Organization, the Karen National Union, the Karenni National Progressive Party, the Kayan New Land Party, the Lahu National United Party, the Palaung State Liberation Party, the Pa-O National Organization, and the Shan State Army.

Party in pursuing dialogue with the Tatmadaw generals or should they maintain their alliance with the NCUB in a joint endeavor to overthrow the regime?

It is a question that the KNU never sufficiently answered. Under constant Tatmadaw attack, the Karen population in refugee camps in Thailand climbed rapidly during the 1990s, passing the 100,000 mark, where it remains today. The consequences for Karen politics and society were far-reaching. Many more Karens simply left their homes to work in Thailand or seek sanctuary in other countries abroad.

For the KNU, however, the most serious blow was a violent rift in 1994–95 that saw the breakaway of the Democratic Karen Buddhist Army (DKBA) in the Hpa-An region. With the DKBA agreeing to a ceasefire with the SLORC government, the Tatmadaw was quickly able to capture Manerplaw and several other KNU strongholds along the Thai border. It was a devastating blow to the KNU's unity and prestige, one that forced Saw Ralph, Naw Sheera, and other veteran leaders to move to refugee camps in Thailand.

Despite the loss of territory, the remaining KNU forces continued to soldier on. All was not lost for the KNU. The military government did not attempt or initiate long-needed processes of reform to bring about nationwide peace, and during the next decade the political contest in the country developed into a tripartite struggle between the Tatmadaw, the NLD, and the different ethnic nationality forces.

Against this backdrop, the pace of change was glacially slow. In 1997, the SLORC renamed itself the State Peace and Development Council (SPDC), but it then took until 2008 for a new constitution to be drawn up that guaranteed to the Tatmadaw the future "leading role" in "national politics." Meanwhile, in 2009, the DKBA was ordered, like other ceasefire groups, to transform into a Border Guard Force (BGF) under Tatmadaw control. But neither the new constitution nor BGF formations appeared to offer any path to inclusive peace and political reform. As the SPDC prepared to hand over office to a quasi-civilian government headed by the ex-general Thein Sein, expectations of meaningful change in the country were very low.

Events now, however, were to move dramatically quickly. In March 2011 the country's new president Thein Sein embarked upon the most rapid period of national reform in over half a century. Political restrictions were lifted, the NLD entered the legislatures in parliamentary by-elections, and in January 2012, amid considerable surprise, the KNU agreed to a ceasefire with the new government. After more than six decades of armed struggle, the KNU was reentering the political mainstream. Optimism about political change then increased when the NLD won the 2015 general election, assuming office the following year. In scenes that once seemed unthinkable, the KNU's long-held objectives of federalism and democracy were publicly promoted by leaders on all sides, including Thein Sein and Aung San Suu Kyi, as the future political direction for the country.

Regrettably, at the time of writing, this is as far as political reform has so far progressed. Substantive political dialogue with the KNU and other ethnic parties has yet to start; armed conflict has resumed in Kachin and Shan States; the Tatmadaw and a Burman-majority elite continue to exert control over many aspects of the economy and government; the 21st Century Panglong Conference, initiated by the NLD government, has failed to bring peace; and Buddhist-Muslim tensions in Rakhine State over the question of Rohingya rights and identity have spiraled into armed conflict and a systematic Tatmadaw crackdown on the Muslim minority.

This latest offensive has resulted in a massive refugee exodus, one of the greatest from any Asian country in recent decades. In August 2018, the United Nations Independent International Fact-Finding Mission on Myanmar recommended that Burma's military leaders be referred to the International Criminal Court for war crimes and crimes against humanity for violations in the Rakhine, Kachin, and Shan States. Many of the condemned tactics are long-standing. Some of this political regression began under the Thein Sein government but, to the disappointment of many international supporters, a number of trends have worsened under the NLD government of Aung San Suu Kyi.

For the Karen people, in contrast, the past seven years have marked a time of relative peace and stability. Long-divided communities have been able to reconnect, expressions of Karen culture and identity have been revived, and attempts have been made to cultivate peace and development in the conflict zones. But, as yet, this upturn does not reflect the situation in the country at large.

As the KNU's founders now pass into history, the political future for both Burma and the KNU is very hard to predict. Karen leaders are anxiously watching the uncertain political landscape to try and ensure that, this time, the Karen people are not left behind during a time of national change. They have already spent too long in the political wilderness. In the meantime, many Karen refugees and displaced persons have yet to return to their homes, and there are concerns among Karen communities on the ground about natural resource exploitation and an inrush of economic projects by outside interests into the country that will not benefit the local people. As the narratives of Saw Ralph and Naw Sheera show, the causes of conflicts in Burma have always been political at root.

We can only hope that, in the immediate future, the present peace and reform processes will come to include the Karens and all the nationalities of Burma. The lessons from history are very clear. Without such participation and inclusion, there will never be peace and stability in the country. After seven decades of armed conflict, Burma's people—from all ethnic backgrounds—have paid a terrible price. National reconciliation and peace remain the greatest tasks facing the country, and this will mean the establishment of a union of equal rights, representation, and justice for all peoples. This was the basis of the modern state that was agreed by the country's leaders at Burma's independence in 1948, and it is long since time that these fundamental rights were respected and guaranteed.

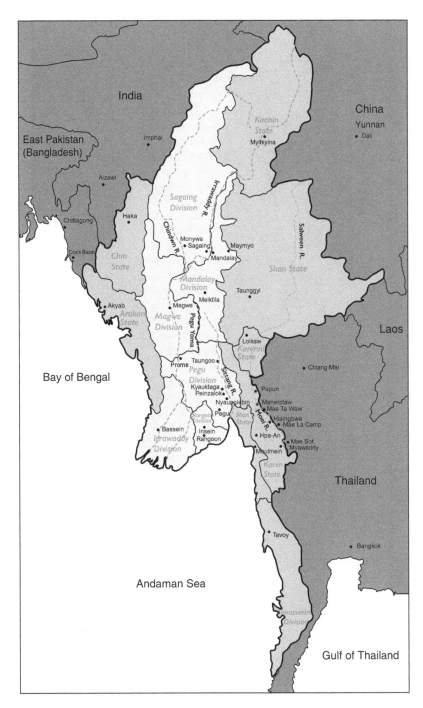

MAP 1. Map of Burma pre-1988

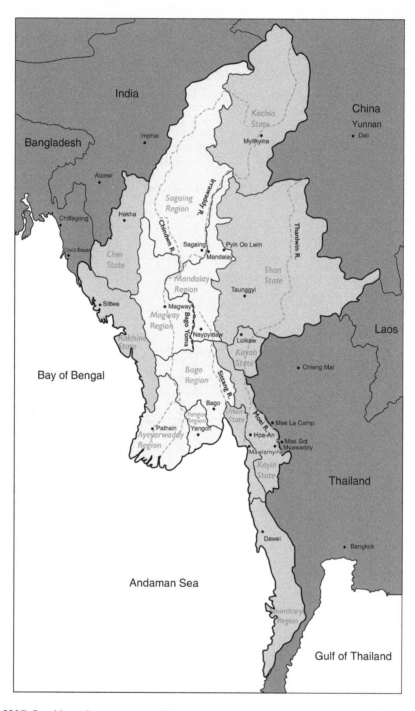

MAP 2. Map of contemporary Myanmar

Part 1
THE SOLDIER
Saw Ralph's Story

EARLY LIFE

When I was a small child, my grandmother would make egg pudding for me. I remember her saying, "If you want pudding, you can go and collect the eggs and I can make pudding for you." Every day I gathered the eggs, and every night she cooked pudding for me. One day she asked me, "Do you like pudding very much?"

"I like it so much I even want to be called Pudding!" I shouted excitedly.

The name stuck, and to this day my brothers and sisters still call me Pudding.

My full name is Ralph Earnest Hodgson. I was named after the English poet Ralph Hodgson who was popular in the 1920s. While I was fighting in the Karen Revolution I just used the name Ralph. I didn't want to put my family in danger, so I didn't dare use my surname. Even when I became a brigadier general I was still Brigadier Ralph or Saw Ralph (Mr. Ralph). Nowadays I am just known as Hpu Ralph (Grandfather Ralph).

Pudding became a code name for me within my family while I was fighting in the revolution. The Burmese authorities and the Karen revolutionaries didn't know who Pudding was, so it was safe for them to talk about me using that name. To further evade detection, my sisters used to refer to me as P. Ding, the brother from Vietnam, in their letters.

I was the eighth of eleven children: Margaret, Jack, Myrtle, Violet, Wilbur, Anne, Edna, me, Maureen, Fanny, and Howard. I also had two older half siblings, Tom and Florence, from my father's first marriage. Two other babies died in infancy.

FIGURE 1. Wedding day of Ralph's parents, John Hodgson and Naw Thet Po, 1919

FIGURE 2.   Ralph (bottom right) with brothers and father (behind)

My father's name was John Farren Hodgson. He worked for the Burma Railways as a permanent way inspector.[1] This meant he was transferred all over Burma building new railways. My paternal grandfather was an English colonial soldier who married my grandmother, a nurse from Arakan. That made my father Anglo-Arakanese. My father was born in Akyab (now Sittwe) in Arakan State in northwest Burma but lived most of his life in Upper Burma, in Mandalay and Sagaing Divisions.[2]

One day, not long after his first wife had passed away, my father accompanied the school inspector Mr. Monroe to a local school in the Peinzalok area where he was stationed. My mother, Naw Thet Po, was sixteen or seventeen years old at the time and a student in the school. Mr. Monroe asked the students in English, "When are lamps lit each evening?" My mother didn't know when the street lamps were lit each evening but she thought she could guess. "6 o'clock!" she answered. Mr. Monroe was blown away. He told my father

---

1. Burma Railways, known as Myanmar Railways today, is the state-owned agency that operates the railway network in Burma. It was first introduced during the British colonial era.

2. Arakan State is known as Rakhine State today. Since Burma's 1974 constitution was put into place, there have been seven divisions (today regions) and seven ethnic states in Burma.

that every school he went to he asked that question and no student could ever answer it. My father looked at her and fell in love.

My father pursued her for a long time. She came from a wealthy hill Karen family who owned a lot of land and elephants. Hill Karens lived in the hills and were often less Burmanized than the plains Karens. My mother came from a long line of Karens and was a typical Karen woman. She was very beautiful and highly educated for a woman in those days—she could read, write, and speak English. Her father thought it was time for her to marry but she took her time choosing from among her many suitors. In the meantime, my father visited her every opportunity he got. He would arrive at the train station outside the village, but to reach it he needed to cross some muddy paddy fields. He didn't want to arrive at my mother's house with dirty clothes so he paid a local farmer one rupee to carry him on his back across the fields.[3] One rupee was a lot of money in those days, so the more my father visited, the wealthier this particular farmer became. Finally, at age twenty-two, my mother married my father.

When they got married, they had a big feast of pork, chicken, duck, and fish curries. There was so much food that everyone forgot the fried catfish sitting in the meat safe.[4] Only after they had finished eating did they find the catfish. They laughed and shared it with all the neighbors. When I was young, my parents would think of their younger days and laugh.

I was born on June 7, 1930, in Monywa in Sagaing Division in northern Burma. During my lifetime I went all over Burma—to Karen State, Karenni State, Shan State, and part of Kachin State—but I never went back to where I was born.[5]

When I was a baby I had a rather protruding head that didn't look normal. My sister Edna, who was only three years old at the time, thought my head was like a coconut. One day she decided she wanted to open the coconut to drink the juice. She found a knife and went to cut open my head. My mother walked out of the bathroom and saw her. "What are you doing!" she screamed and slapped her. I was very lucky because if my mother hadn't walked in, Edna would have killed me.

My family was privileged, and we lived in a big three-story house. The ground floor was stone with two wooden floors above. In those days a government salary could support a whole family, so my mother never worked, and we lived

---

3. The Indian rupee was used in Burma during British colonization until it became a separate British colony in 1937. The current currency, called the kyat, was introduced in 1952, and was also used prior to British colonization.

4. A "meat safe" is a meshed food pantry still used by households in Burma that cannot afford a refrigerator.

5. Karenni State is known as Kayah State today.

comfortably. My mother also inherited a large number of paddy fields from her father and bought more fields with their extra money. They owned over two hundred acres of paddy fields. At that time Burma was the rice bowl of Asia, with enough rice for everyone plus for export. Those who didn't own their own land could work other people's land and earn enough to live on. My father intended to retire on the income from our paddy fields.

My mother's parents used to come down from the hills to the plains to visit us for weeks at a time. They were Christian but they didn't speak English. My mother had two brothers and six sisters who were all fond of music—playing piano and violin and writing songs. We were close to my two uncles and my aunties who were very good at sewing and knitting. My eldest aunt didn't come down from the hills to visit us, so we used to go and visit her. Another aunt—a beautiful, fair Karen—died from tuberculosis when she was eighteen years old. There were many Karens around where we lived in Peinzalok, so my mother had many family and friends around, and there were a lot of cousins for us to play with.

My mother was a Baptist and my father a Methodist.[6] When I was young we went to church, and we listened to what they told us, but we didn't understand much. We just went for the sake of attending church.

My brothers and sisters and I all attended the same schools. Starting at age five we all attended day school at the American Baptist Mission School (ABM School) in Meiktila and then at age seven, we moved to the ABM School in Moulmein, a boarding school.[7] Our parents sent us to the ABM School in Moulmein because it had high academic standards, but as it was actually a girls' school, we boys could only attend the primary school. After that my brothers attended a Baptist English High School. The ABM School in Moulmein went up to the tenth standard for girls, so my sisters continued at this school until after the tenth standard, when they went to Judson College in Rangoon to study English.

Each year we traveled by train to school for one day and one night, a trip that today would only take a few hours. We changed trains at Pegu and then went on to Martaban.[8] My father would arrange second-class tickets so we would have beds, but while we waited at Pegu we would sleep on the station benches. Then we slept until we had to wake up and take the ferry across the Salween River

---

6. Some of the earliest Christian missionary work in Burma took place among the Karen people in the delta. Today, approximately 20 percent of Karens are Christian, with the remaining Karens Buddhists or animists (Thawnghmung 2008: 3).

7. Moulmein is known as Mawlamyine today and is the capital of Mon State. It was also the first capital of British Burma between 1826 and 1852.

8. Pegu is known as Bago today and is the capital of Bago Region.

to Moulmein. Every time we traveled back to school we would cry because we would get homesick. But once we saw our school friends we would quickly forget our homesickness. I liked school when I was young.

Because the British ruled Burma and I went to a Baptist missionary school, English was compulsory and the language of instruction at my primary school.[9] So, all of us learned English very well. My primary school didn't teach Burmese and in the first year of school, we were fined one anna for each Burmese word we spoke.[10] After the second year, we became a little more fluent in English. By the third year, we had no problem speaking English and when we went home we couldn't find the Burmese words we wanted to use. At home we spoke a mix of English and Burmese with my parents. We understood Sgaw Karen but we couldn't reply in Karen, so we had to reply in Burmese or English.[11]

By blood, I am Karen-Anglo-Arakanese. I consider myself a Karen, but the first language I spoke was Burmese because my father was working all over Burma speaking Burmese. My father didn't speak Sgaw Karen, but he could understand if someone was talking about him. I never studied Karen history at school, because at primary school they taught us English history, and after the war and Burma's independence, we studied Burmese history. Our Karen relatives used to tell us stories; they call it *hta* in Karen, meaning poetry. They recited the stories because there were no books. At bedtime our mothers told us these stories. Our uncles and aunts also used to tell us stories. My own children grew up in Karen villages, so they learned the Karen languages and Karen history and stories in school. In some ways they know more about our Karen heritage than I do.

During the summer holidays, my siblings and I would all come home from boarding school. When we reunited for the break, the house was full of joy, and there was always a lot of noise and laughter. My mother would play the piano, and we would all sing. In the afternoon she would rest with the smallest baby. My sisters could sing and play the piano too. My father had an office out back where my brothers and I would go and play to annoy him. We wanted him to shout at us. We had nannies, but nobody could control us. I was close to both my mother

---

9. During the colonial period, the British administration also established bilingual Anglo-vernacular schools that taught in both English and Burmese, while the Buddhist Sanga continued to teach in monasteries in Burmese (Cheesman 2003: 50-51).

10. Anna was a currency unit equal to a sixteenth of a rupee.

11. The Sgaw Karen language, spoken by Ralph and his mother's family, is one of the Karen languages spoken in Burma and Thailand. The British colonial authorities identified twenty-one Karen subgroups, including Sgaw, Pwo, Kayah, Kayan, and Pa-O. The Sgaw and Pwo Karens are the two largest groups, constituting 65 percent of the Karen-related population. In addition, the KNU has historically been dominated by these two groups (Thawnghmung 2012). The Karen Christian population primarily consists of Sgaw Karens, while the Pwo Karens are mainly Buddhists and animists.

and father. Every night my brothers and sisters and I would massage our father until he fell asleep. In Burma they tell children to come inside when it gets dark or the ghosts will get us. They frightened us to keep us quiet, but from that time on I was afraid of ghosts.

My relationships with my siblings were all different. There were big age gaps between the youngest and the oldest siblings. My sister Margaret and Florence, my eldest half-sister, were like mothers to me. My eldest half-brother moved away to Upper Burma to run a livestock farm. He had always been interested in farming, so my father bought him a farm. My siblings were all friendly and never mean. Myrtle was always helping while everyone loved Violet because she had a good sense of humor.

When I was young I had lots of friends of all sorts; we also had toys but only until primary school. We sometimes played the Burmese game *chinlone,* where four or five players try to keep a rattan ball aloft by kicking it or by using other parts of your body. Football was another favorite. My parents told me to play in the house, but I would always go outside, and my skin would get darker and darker, so my siblings called me the black sheep.

My father had a brother who was also a railway inspector. He also had a sister who taught at the ABM school in Moulmein. My uncle Arthur Hodgson constructed the railway line from Moulmein to Ye. He lived ten miles from Moulmein, and on Friday evenings he would come to collect us from school and send us back on Sunday evenings. The food at the school was tough for us, as we had to eat whatever they fed us. So when we went to my uncle's home for the weekends, his cook made us whatever we wanted to eat. We could eat all day.

The teachers ate in the same dining hall, but they had better food. The teachers would ask us to shine their shoes for them in exchange for some of their better food. At night the students would only get bread and butter. But if you shined the teachers' shoes, they would give you ice cream or pudding. Some boys didn't want to do it because they thought it was a dirty job. I didn't mind because I wanted to eat the pudding!

When my uncle was busy on Fridays, he would ask his cook to come and meet us at school. His cook was a short, stout Indo-Burman man. Once, when he was waiting in the sitting room next to the principal's office, the principal asked what this stranger was doing there. Some of the other students knew him so they told my sisters that the cook was there to meet them. One of my elder sisters, Violet, came to meet the cook. The principal asked her who the gentleman was, and Violet, who was a real character, casually replied, "Oh, he's my boy." We called the cooks and servants "boy," but it seemed to mean something else to the principal. The cook was a little older than my uncle, so the principal was shocked. Then people started teasing Violet. The next time the cook came, they said, "Violet, your boy is here!"

People liked British rule because everything was systematic.[12] Many people in Burma were happy under the British, but some Burmese didn't like the British and wanted to rule their own country. Starting from Burma's independence, the country went from bad to worse, day by day, year by year. When the military took power, everything got worse.

In the days of British rule, people were excited when they saw airplanes. During Burmese military rule, many Karens left by plane, heading to Australia, America, Norway, or Sweden—all over the world. If it weren't for the Burmese military, we would still be in Burma living the same life, generation after generation.[13] Now everyone is spread all over the world. We were like frogs that had fallen in a well. We thought the world was only as much as we could see from the bottom of the well. Yet when we arrived in different countries, it was like the frog had been pulled out of the well and could see the world was bigger.

---

12. Karens, along with other minorities in British Burma, generally received preferential treatment under the colonial government. Karens served in the military and police forces during colonial rule and remained loyal to the British, even during the Japanese occupation of Burma (Morrison 1947; Smith 1999; Kratoska 2002).

13. Burma was a parliamentary democracy between the country's independence from Britain in 1948 and the coup d'état led by General Ne Win in 1962. Following the coup, the armed forces led the government until a quasi-civilian parliamentary system was implemented in 2011.

JAPANESE OCCUPATION

In 1941 a group of nationalist leaders known as the Thirty Comrades, led by General Aung San, went to Japan to receive military training and weapons.[1] The Thirty Comrades wanted to gain independence from the British, so they recruited a small army of mostly Burman men and formed the Burma Independence Army (BIA). With Britain and its allies occupied on the Western Front in Europe, the Japanese started invading other countries in Asia. With support from the Thirty Comrades and their new army, the Japanese invaded Burma in 1942.[2] The British didn't have any reinforcements to defend Burma, so they couldn't stop the Japanese offensive. The British troops started withdrawing and the villagers fled into the jungle. Within a week we saw Japanese soldiers pouring in. Before long they had taken over the whole country. There were air raids by the British over towns and the countryside; the British planes also harassed the Japanese lines of communication along the land and river routes.

I was eleven years old when the Japanese invaded. At the time, our house was close to the railway line at Peinzalok. The town was on the Rangoon-Mandalay main road, making it a target for the Japanese, so our family evacuated to the

---

1. Aung San is considered the father of modern Burma and is the founder of the Tatmadaw, the Burmese armed forces. He is also the father of the Nobel Peace Prize laureate Aung San Suu Kyi.

2. According to Martin Smith, the entry of the BIA "received a rapturous reception from the Burman majority. Most of Burma's ethnic minorities, however, remained ominously silent" (Smith 1999, 59).

jungle with the rest of our village. Fortunately, my parents were home at the time. We had to run with just the clothes on our backs and we went to the jungle to stay with my mother's Karen relatives.

My mother was afraid because my sisters were teenagers and the Japanese were notorious for raping young women. When we were hiding in the jungle my sisters were so scared at night they couldn't sleep. They slept with my mother on a big mat on the floor. My mother would pinch them to make sure they were awake so if the Japanese came in the middle of the night they could run.

For me, life in the jungle as a teenage boy was an adventure. I loved living in the remote areas of the jungle. It was quite hot in the summer, so my brothers and sisters and I spent all day at a nearby lake. We would dive under the water, feeling for the fish and catching them with our bare hands. Sometimes we went fishing in the mud where we would use a hook to scratch in the ground or we would throw in a net.

From our childhood we had schooling but knew nothing of jungle life. While we lived in the jungle, my siblings and I learned how to find seasonal fruit and vegetables. The Karen villagers and my mother's family taught us how to survive in the jungle. Every day in the jungle we used a slingshot to shoot birds and eat them. With the fish, birds, and wild fruit and vegetables, we had plenty of food. Some villagers grew their own vegetables but also picked wild plants. We also learned more Karen language. Learning to survive in the jungle was like school and I enjoyed it very much.

When the British retreated, my whole family went to the hills together except my eldest sister, Margaret, who was in Upper Burma with her husband, Moses. We stayed in the jungle for a few months during the invasion, but once the Japanese had occupied the whole of Burma, my family returned to our home in Peinzalok, and Margaret went back to Rangoon with her husband. The schools were closed, so we all stayed at home with our parents. My mother was still afraid for my sisters, so she tried to keep them inside, away from the Japanese soldiers.

During the Japanese occupation our parents had a very difficult time and were often worried. The cost of living was very high, so they had to sell their jewels and cattle so that we would have money for food.

My parents had bought some buffalo and cows that our relatives looked after for us. When we came back from the jungle, I asked my parents to take back some of the buffalo and cows because I wanted to look after them.

They brought back four buffalo bulls and some cows. Every day the buffalo would go to different villages because they were all males looking for female buffalo. In the evening I had to get them back one by one, so I would go on foot to the furthest village, catch a buffalo, ride it back, tie it up and then keep going back for the others until it was dark. Sometimes it was dark and I couldn't find some of them. I even cried, but I knew it was my fault because I had asked my parents to bring the buffalo back and I dared not tell them I was unhappy. Eventually, they decided to sell them and asked me if I would agree. I was so happy to get rid of them! From then on, I just looked after the cows.

Not long after we returned to the village my mother became ill. She had stomach ulcers that caused her great pain and vomiting. There were no hospitals or medical supplies available because of the Japanese occupation. A doctor used to give her pink pills but that didn't help much. We all knew she was dying.

She loved all her children and wanted us all around her when she passed away. I didn't want to see her die or see her struggling at the end. I didn't want to remember her like that so I ran to the neighbor's house. My family keep calling out for me to come back but I stayed hidden and didn't go back until the next day. They told me there was no need to go back because my mother was gone now.

I was just a young boy and I didn't fully understand what was happening. My father felt sad because he had lost a wife for a second time. He also pitied us children because he knew he could not look after us like our mother.

They buried my mother between two tombs in the paddy field. A lot of people came and many were crying at her funeral. I didn't cry then, only afterwards. In Karen culture it's ok to cry. The first dead body I saw was my mother's. Later in life I saw so many dead bodies that it became a normal sight.

My uncle Arthur, whom we stayed with on weekends while we were at boarding school, also passed away during the Japanese occupation. He was a heavy smoker and died of tuberculosis. There weren't any hospitals, so he didn't have the chance to cure himself either.

After my mother's death I went to stay with Margaret, who was living with her husband in Rangoon. As they didn't yet have any children, she wanted some of her siblings to stay with her. I had heard there were often air raids in Rangoon and I wanted to see a real raid, so I agreed to go.

Margaret's husband, Moses, was the second highest Scout Master in Burma.[3] They lived in a house in the Scouts' compound on Inya Lake. One evening in the hot season I went to bathe in the lake and saw something moving in the clouds. I was frightened and ran back to Margaret's house. I said, "Margaret, Margaret, look at the sky! There are angels!"

"Where are the angels?" She asked.

I told her what I'd seen. She laughed and told me they were searchlights. I'd never seen clouds look like that before. The searchlights made them look extraordinary.

---

3. A Scout Master was the adult leader of a group of boys in the Burmese scout movement.

When the British planes came, the Japanese started searching the skies. There was an antiaircraft gun near Margaret's house just beyond the lake. The noise from the antiaircraft gun was powerful and unforgettable.

Flossie Lao, Eric Wong, and Major Mitsu

Margaret had a friend called Flossie Lao who had studied with my sisters at the ABM School in Moulmein. She was a beautiful Sino-Burmese lady, well educated and from a good middle-class family. In 1942 she became engaged to Lieutenant Eric Wong, who served in the British army and was a friend of my brother-in-law Moses. He was also half Chinese and a good-hearted man.

When the British forces withdrew to India, Flossie thought Eric had gone to India with the British army, but he had stayed behind in Upper Burma. When the Japanese occupied Burma, Flossie met a Japanese officer called Major Mitsu at the Japanese broadcasting station where she worked. The major had five blue stars, meaning he was in the administration and not a fighting man. He was kind and polite with children like me. Both Eric and Mitsu loved the same woman, but they didn't know about each other.

Sometime later, Eric Wong came back to Rangoon, went straight to Flossie's house, and called out to her from downstairs as soon as he arrived. She was so shocked to hear his voice and answered him as she ran out on to the upstairs veranda. But the veranda was old and rickety and it collapsed as she ran. She fell to the ground below. Eric rushed her to the hospital. He cared for her for about a month until she passed away.

Major Mitsu came to see her and Eric told him that she had passed away. Both Eric and Major Mitsu wanted to visit her family to comfort them. Her family lived next door to Margaret's house on Inya Lake, so they asked Moses to arrange a boat to take them from the marketplace to Flossie's parents' house. Moses arranged for an Indian man to take them.

That day Moses and I were weeding in the garden facing the lake. I saw a boat with three people coming toward us from a faraway market place. I didn't pay much attention and kept on weeding. Suddenly I heard someone shouting for help. When I looked up I saw the boat sinking. One person was helping to drag the other person who could not swim, attempting to save his life. The person who had been rowing the boat clung to a basket. Someone was still shouting for help when Moses heard, looked toward the lake and told me to quickly get one of the canoes. We both hurried and rowed toward them. By the time we were halfway out, two of the men had already disappeared below the water. When we got there, we couldn't find the place where they went under. We were only able to rescue the Indian boat driver, who clung to a floating basket of books. The other two men drowned.

Their bodies floated up the next day and we went to fetch their corpses. Only then could we identify them as Eric Wong, a British Lieutenant, and Major Mitsu from the Nippon Imperial Army. Eric had tried to save Mitsu who couldn't swim with his uniform and tall boots on. The Japanese military police, the Kempeitai, came and interrogated Moses and me before they took the corpses away.

At the time, I didn't really understand life and death. I thought what was happening was fun. Moses got very angry with me. He only discovered they were drowning when he heard Eric shouting for help, whereas I'd seen them coming all the way from the marketplace. I'd started laughing when I saw the Indian man swimming on a basket full of books. Moses couldn't get over this incident. He felt guilty because he was the one who sent the boat to collect them. It was a very serious situation, but I thought it was funny. I was too childish and ignorant to understand the seriousness of the situation.

Kyauktaga Railway Station

In 1944 I returned to Peinzalok and took a job at the Kyauktaga railway station as a ticket collector.[4] I was only fourteen years old but I felt I was older than I was. I got the job because my uncle Maung Tin, Aunty Mae's husband, was an assistant stationmaster. There were three stationmasters: two were Burmese and one was an officer from the Japanese army. There were about seven Japanese soldiers posted there. One of the station staff had to be near the phone at all times in case he had to sound the air raid alarm. There were trains coming day and night, so we were on duty twenty-four hours a day. I slept at the station in the staff living quarters with all the other staff.

I was very friendly with the Japanese stationmaster. His name was Kondo-san.[5] He said that we boys who worked at the station reminded him of his sons. In the evenings, sitting outside where it was cool, he had taught us Japanese songs. I can still remember a little Japanese, even seventy years later. None of my brothers or sisters worked with the Japanese. Everything I did was different from my brothers and sisters in one way or another.

On March 27, 1945, it was very hot. At about eight o'clock in the evening, a friend and I went onto an overhead railway bridge to feel the cool breeze.

---

4. Kyauktaga railway station is in Pegu District on the Rangoon-Mandalay line.
5. "San" is a Japanese honorific of respect.

My friend was a deserter from the Japanese Heho Unit. He could speak a little Japanese because in the Heho Unit, if you said any little thing wrong, you would get slapped. He was slapped every day, so he ran away. Any song I could think of, he could sing. So, we lay down in the moonlight and started singing. Suddenly we saw a British airplane circling above. It bombed and strafed the town quarters.[6] We thought we saw some paratroopers drop to attack the Japanese.

Suddenly we heard two rounds of rifle fire at the Japanese stationmaster's quarters. The Burmese stationmaster called out to me to go and see what had happened. I ran toward the gunfire with two other boys, one Burmese and one Indian. On my way I found a group of Burma National Army (BNA) soldiers.[7] They were not paratroopers and a British plane hadn't dropped them. I realized each group was implementing their own plan and the BNA soldiers had turned against the Japanese. The BNA soldiers had shot our Japanese stationmaster and were hastily withdrawing. They called out asking who the three of us were. I gave them no answer and ran to the Japanese officer. He was struggling for breath. A few seconds later, he was silent.

I pitied the Japanese stationmaster because we had been very friendly with him. He treated us like his sons in Japan; he loved us, and we loved him. When he died, we felt very sad even though we were related only through our friendship. His family didn't know he was gone; we didn't know where his family was living or how to communicate with them. We worried: how will they know what happened to him?

If we had been with the stationmaster that evening, we probably would have been killed too. All over Burma the Japanese used young boys like us as interpreters. The Japanese taught the brighter ones to collect information for them. The parents didn't know that their children were working for the enemy. The Japanese didn't ask adults to collect information because they would have only given them some information and withheld the most important parts. These children were much hated by the population, and the BNA soldiers would have felt the same. But we were not involved politically, nor did we give information. We were only working at the railway station to aid transportation.

---

6. "Strafe" is a technical military term describing an attack in which a low-flying aircraft repeatedly sweeps the ground below with machine-gun fire.

7. After the Japanese invaded Burma, the Burma Independence Army was eventually disbanded. In its place, the Japanese created the Burma Defence Army (BDA), under the command of General Aung San, along with organizations designed to guide Burma toward independence. When Burma was granted nominal independence by Japan in the summer of 1943, the army was renamed the Burma National Army (BNA).

I went back and reported to the Burmese stationmaster. He asked all of us to abandon the place and go home. The Indian boy was afraid to go home alone, so he followed me. We set off to the village where my aunty lived. In the deserted town, at the headman's house, there were BNA officers discussing the situation. Everything was dark, but the light was on at the headman's house. Just before we reached the house, a sentry challenged us, asking who we were. He took us to the headman's house to check whether he knew us or if we were working for the Japanese. When we got there we found we also knew one of the Burmese stationmasters. The stationmaster and the headman discouraged us from going to my aunt's village because it was dark, so we decided to sleep at the headman's house.

In the middle of the night, the Indian boy woke me up. Panicked, he said, "There's nobody here! I don't know where everybody has gone!" I woke up and looked around, but nobody was there. I was scared, but dared not go out because anybody could shoot us. We couldn't sleep any more in this critical situation and determined to leave at dawn.

But just as the sun rose, the Japanese troops' special train rolled into the town with lots of troops and a convoy of military trucks. They quickly took over the town. They came searching, flashing their torchlights here and there, looking for the headman's house. When they reached the house, they shouted "*Bee ru ma, Bee ru ma!*" (Burmese, Burmese!)

We had no escape, and at first, we dared not answer them. Then we thought: it doesn't matter, we'll answer them. They told us to open the door, but we were locked in. We told them, so they shot the lock open and took us to the Kempeitai, the Japanese intelligence unit, where we were interviewed by a colonel. We told them exactly what had happened. Fortunately, we still had our station armbands on.

The soldiers took us back to the station, where three of the adult railway staff had already been captured by the Japanese on their way home. The trains were no longer running, so we had nothing to do. We were thinking: how do we sneak out? There were too many Japanese soldiers, so we just stayed and waited, for one or two days.

The Japanese soldiers had also thought it had been British paratroopers until they heard from us. Then their headquarters informed them that the Japanese had been attacked throughout the whole of Burma. Only then did we learn that Aung San and his troops had turned against the Japanese.

The commander asked us all, "Who can speak Japanese?" The majority answered that they could. The commander sent one soldier over to get the Indian boy and me and interviewed us about the Japanese stationmaster. They asked us how we felt. I replied, "We feel very sad because he was friendly with us."

The commander trusted us. He asked us if we knew any villages on the outskirts of the town. I told him that my uncle's and my aunt's village was around here.

He told me to go to the village and collect information for them. At first, I thought that I dared not do what they were asking. Then, suddenly, I thought that would be a good way to get out of here!

I told the commander that I would do it but that I would also like to take the Indian boy with me because I was too scared to travel alone. They taught us how to collect information and gave me a movement order and a recommendation paper. When we were leaving, our friends who had to stay behind pleaded with us to return. They were afraid no one would come back for them and they would be slaughtered. I promised them that if I was not captured by any troops, I would return.

We left Kyauktaga town, walked about one thousand yards, and stopped at a Japanese observation post. We showed them our papers and were passed through. We walked another three miles and arrived at Payagyigon village, where my Aunty Mae and her husband and children were living. They asked us, "Are you going back to your father's house?"

"I don't know" I replied.

"You can't stay here," they told me. "Go back to your father, brothers, and sisters so you are all together."

I didn't want to go back because I wanted to understand the situation more. I had a feeling the British were reoccupying these places and then the real changes would happen. If I stayed, I could watch the British defeat the Japanese. Then I could go home and boast to my brothers and sisters, telling them how it happened. But my aunty told me not to go back to the Japanese because, she said, the situation was not good. She told me, "In a few days, the British will be back and the fighting will start, so you'd better go back to your parents now." I still wanted to go back to the Japanese. I thought that even if the British captured us, they wouldn't kill us, and then at least I would know the whole story. I didn't tell my aunt that I was going back to the Japanese and just went off with the Indian boy.

The British had dropped arms and ammunition in the Karen areas. They recruited and armed Karen levies to fight the Japanese who were scattered after the battle by guerrilla warfare. After walking three hundred yards from the village we came across the Karen levies known as the Force 136 Spider Group. One of my cousins was in the group and he told me not to go back to the Japanese because tomorrow or the day after the British would reoccupy this whole area. I told him I wanted to go back but he insisted that I go back to my father.

He told the Indian boy to go back to his village. So, we parted ways and I headed back to my village. After walking for several hours, I got home safely to a nearby village where my father, brothers, and sisters had been evacuated from Peinzalok. I was safe from combat.

The next morning the tanks rolled in, but we didn't know whose tanks they were. We were far from the town, with no communications. I thought it was the

Japanese who were retreating but actually it was the British who were advancing. I was happy the British had come back. Later on, I thought to myself that I was lucky I didn't go back to the Japanese because they would have used me as an interpreter and dragged me along in their retreat out of Burma.

I think the Japanese used the rest of my friends from the station to collect information. Like me, my friends wouldn't have returned to the Japanese, but would have taken opportunities to escape and would have survived.

In those days I didn't know how to be afraid. I just wanted adventure and something to brag about. My family was very happy when I returned. They had been anxious that I might be stupid and stick with the Japanese because we were very friendly with the Japanese stationmaster. They were afraid I had no chance of survival.

The Japanese were forced to retreat as the tides of war gradually changed against them. By 1944 Aung San had approached the Allies and engineered a deal that would allow him and the Thirty Comrades a pivotal role in a newly independent Burma. They formed the Anti-Fascist Organization (AFO) as a resistance movement against the Japanese occupation. At first the Burmese supported the Japanese invasion but later they turned on the Japanese. During the war, which side the Burmese supported depended on the situation.

The Karens, in contrast, had experienced a number of atrocities during the Japanese occupation, especially in the Delta region, because they had mostly remained loyal to the British throughout the war. Throughout the Japanese occupation my mother hoped the British would return. All the time she prayed for the British to reoccupy Burma. In the evening, the whole family would have a night service before bed. Each night we all had to pray in turn for the British to return. She said that if she saw the British return, it wouldn't matter that she died. But she never got to see them return.

The Japanese occupation was both a good time and a bad time in my life. We children liked the Japanese occupation because the occupying forces taught us the Japanese language and Japanese songs and they also engaged with us. The adults didn't like this because they were anti-Japanese and they preferred the British. We children liked those who were in front of our eyes, not those we couldn't see.

Postwar Burma

After the Japanese left, life went back to as it was before the war, except my mother was gone. When the British reoccupied Burma I stayed with my father for a short time. I then returned to Rangoon to stay with my sister Margaret. I attended the

Chettiar Residential High School in Rangoon.[8] I studied there because it was close to Margaret's house. I liked the school. My friends were children from all different races—Chettiar, Burmese, Chinese.

I stayed as a boarder at the Chettiar School for one year because I didn't want to walk to school every day. The following year I changed my mind and went to live with Margaret even though I had to walk to school. At school, they taught English and Tamil but no Burmese. I liked it because Burmese was hard for me. In other schools I had to take beginning Burmese, but at the Chettiar School there was no one to teach it. In the other schools, if you passed your other subjects but didn't pass Burmese, you didn't pass. In the Chettiar School, as long as you passed English, you were ok. I wanted to study the Tamil language and attended Tamil classes for two or three days. The teachers would slap you if you couldn't pronounce the words properly. But if they slapped my face like that it would go bright red. I thought I'd better give up before it became a big problem.

After Burma became independent from the British on January 4, 1948, and the Anti-Fascist People's Freedom League (AFPFL) took over, the political situation got much worse in Burma.[9] Privately owned land was confiscated from landowners and redistributed. My father dared not try to stop them, so he lost all his thirty acres of rice paddy. My father had to go stay in Rangoon and Insein, a town about nine miles from Rangoon, instead.

There was no security in the countryside for my father and siblings, so the family was broken up. Maureen, Fanny, Howard, Myrtle, and I lived with my sister Margaret at Inya Road in Rangoon. My sisters Anne and Edna lived in Insein with my half sister Florence and her family. From there, Edna and Anne traveled by train to work in Rangoon every day. Violet worked as a nurse at Rangoon General Hospital.

Two of my brothers, Jack and Wilbur, joined the Burmese armed forces after the Japanese occupation. My eldest brother, Jack, studied engineering and, after he graduated, joined the Burma Engineers. Wilbur got married and had a son. Wilbur was an ordinance officer in the Quartermaster's Branch stationed in Rangoon.

---

8. Chettiars are a cast originally from Tamil Nadu in southern India. Chettiars moved to Burma en masse during British colonial rule and were influential in the Burmese economy. Chettiars were widely resented by Burmans for their roles as moneylenders and for their close association with colonial rule (Turnell 2009: 13-52). During the 1930s, there were several pogroms against the Indian community in Burma, including the Chettiars.

9. The AFO had evolved into the Anti-Fascist People's Freedom League (AFPFL), the main political alliance in Burma from 1945 until 1958. The AFPFL included the Communist Party of Burma (CPB), the Burma National Army, and the People's Revolutionary Party, which later evolved into the Socialist Party. The AFPFL became the de facto successor government of Burma and negotiated with the British for independence and with the ethnic minorities in forming an alliance. Eventually an internal split developed within the AFPFL and, soon after Burma became independent, the CPB launched an armed insurgency against the AFPFL government.

When I graduated from high school I applied to be an apprentice at the Burma Locomotive Railway Workshop where my half-sister Florence's husband, Harold, was a foreman. Harold had quit the Catholic priesthood so he could marry Florence. He got a job as a foreman in the railway workshop and they had six children.

In 1947 I moved to Insein and started my apprenticeship. Before this time, it had been very hard to apply for apprenticeships. I was very lucky because after independence there was a lack of skilled workers. Many of the Indians had left after independence and workers were needed to fill their places. As I was Harold's brother-in-law, it was very easy for me to get an apprenticeship. As part of my apprenticeship I had to work at the workshop and attend two hours of theory classes nightly at the BOC College of Engineering and Mining.[10] Doing practical work and studying theory was very tiring, but at least I could speak to my brother Jack about our engineering studies.

After completing my engineering studies, I would become a boiler inspector. I was quite happy about this because under the British, engineers would normally have had to work at least ten years to get a boiler inspector position, but since there were so many vacancies, I expected to finish my apprenticeship the following year. But the civil war broke out and my life and career path forever changed.

---

10. The college was name after the Burmah Oil Company and is now part of Yangon Technical University.

THE REVOLUTION BEGINS

When I first started at the locomotive workshop in Insein, my Burmese colleagues were friendly, and we respected one another. But as the political situation destabilized, slowly the Burmese workers changed. After they undertook basic training in the local Burmese militia defense groups, known as the Burmese Territorial Forces (*Sitwundan* in Burmese), my Burmese colleagues began talking and acting differently. They started to treat the Karen workers differently and stopped being friendly. They would come to work armed and in their militia uniforms. They became proud and bossy, which made all of the other workers unhappy to be around them. We could not bear their behavior and just looked at them out of the corners of our eyes. There is a Burmese saying that when someone is armed with weapons, he is "like a horse with horns. No matter how you approach him—from the front legs, the hind legs, or the horns—he will attack you." I began to realize that trouble lay ahead.

With tensions in Insein at a boiling point, a number of supposedly coincidental events happened. At Karen New Year on December 29, 1948, a number of bursts of rifle fire and automatic gunfire were directed at the Karen quarters in Insein. In the Karen quarters in Thamaing, a town between Rangoon and Insein on the Rangoon-Insein road, similar incidents were reported, including indiscriminate mortar fire. When there was fighting in Thamaing, we could not travel between Rangoon and Insein. This continued throughout January 1949. One report stated that a Territorial Forces armored car had indiscriminately fired into areas populated by Karens. Fearful that there would be a sudden outbreak of fighting, General Smith Dun, a Karen who was the first commander in chief of the Burma National Army at independence, approached Prime Minister U Nu to arrange a meeting with Saw Ba U Gyi, the leader of the Karen National Union (KNU).[1] The meeting was an attempt to quell the rising tensions. U Nu agreed, and a meeting was scheduled for January 31, 1949, at noon.

I was engaged to a young Karen nurse called E Aye at the time. We called her Baby. She worked at the Rangoon General Hospital. She was two years younger than I. The night before the meeting was scheduled to occur, I took the train to Rangoon to visit her. She was worried that fighting would break out between the Burmese and the Karens, and worried that if fighting broke out I would join the fight—and she would end up having to marry a Burmese man. She told me that if fighting started I should come and meet her at once, and she would leave her job and come with me. She said, "Don't leave without me!" I reassured her that everything would be fine and then took the last train back to Insein. After my train, all transportation between Rangoon and Insein was stopped. I couldn't go back to get Baby and it would be many decades until I saw her again.

The next morning Thamaing and Insein were surrounded and attacked by the Territorial Forces, causing a number of casualties. The outnumbered Karens were able to hold out until reinforcements from the Karen National Defence Organisation (KNDO) were able to beat back the attackers.[2] With open hostilities now taking place, more KNDO units were placed on alert. They arrived in Insein and attacked the Territorial Forces positions, forcing their retreat to the Insein jail and a nearby rice mill on the Hlaing River.

---

1. On February 5, 1947, with the impending independence of Burma, several Karen organizations came together to form the Karen National Union with the goal of safeguarding Karen interests (Smith 1999, 45, 83). They included the Karen National Association (KNA), Baptist KNA, Buddhist KNA, Karen Central Organisation, and its youth wing, the Karen Youth Organisation. The oldest was the KNA, which had been set up in 1881 by Christian Karens to promote identity and progress among all Karens, regardless of religion or location. The KNU, however, was marginalized in the countdown to the British departure. Karen representatives did not take part in the Panglong Conference of February 1947 that agreed on the principles of equality and ethnic autonomy for the future Union of Burma, and the KNU boycotted elections to the Constituent Assembly later that year. These events laid the platform for divisions in Karen politics that are yet to be resolved. Saw Ba U Gyi was the first president of the Karen National Union. He was educated at the University of Cambridge and, after he passed the English bar, he returned to Burma. During the Second World War, he associated with Aung San and the AFO, seeking to improve Burmese-Karen relations, and he was a cabinet minister in the preindependence government after the Second World War ended. Alongside his government work, he also advocated for the establishment of an independent Karen state. He was one of the Karen delegates in a four-man "Goodwill Delegation" of lawyers who traveled to London in August 1946 to solicit British support for Karen political aspirations. He eventually led the KNU into armed struggle in January 1949.

2. The KNDO, founded in 1947, is one of the armed wings of the KNU. It is utilized primarily as a defensive force for Karen villages.

I could see the Karen quarters from the railway workshop. I saw Burmese soldiers appear on the oval in front of the seminary school and begin to fire into the Karen quarters using mortars and small arms. The gunfire continued throughout the day, and in the evening the battle started. The Karen workers were told by Karen soldiers to leave the workshop and go back to the seminary school. That same day the Karen soldiers occupied the Karen quarters and the locomotive workshop and liberated the Insein jail. The locomotive workshop was suddenly the middle of a battlefield.

At dawn the Karen fighters launched a counterattack on the Burmese soldiers. The Karens were prepared with arms and jeeps under the primary school at the seminary. The Burmese forces set fire to the buildings to stop the Karen forces from advancing. However, the fire spread quickly until the whole town was ablaze. When the fire died down, the Territorial Forces retreated to the rice mill near the river and withdrew by boat.

During all of this, none of the Karen workers went to work. My sister Florence and her six children, my siblings Edna, Fanny, Maureen, and Howard, and I were all moved to the house of Rayleigh Dee, the husband of our mother's cousin. He lived at the local seminary school and was the editor of a Karen Christian magazine where he published Karen hymns.

On the way, we saw chaos all around. We saw Karens in jeeps shooting. We saw prisoners that we recognized from the jail, including Captain Vivian, who had been a British officer in the Royal Army Ordinance Corps, in charge of military equipment. He had been arrested for supplying the Bren guns that were used for the assassination of General Aung San and most of his cabinet in 1947. U Saw, a prewar prime minister and the architect of the assassination, was executed, and Captain Vivian was given a two-year sentence in the Insein jail. The Karens released him from the jail and hoped that he would help them get more arms and ammunition.

The seminary was a big compound with different schools and a football field. There were thirteen of us staying in one house in the seminary grounds. I was staying in the servants' quarters next to the house. We dug a trench outside the house to hide from the shelling. The shells landed eight or ten feet away from where we were sleeping, leaving small craters. It was so scary. One day our cook went out to the toilet, which was separate from the house. When he came back he couldn't speak. He just made a noise. Later on he told us the bomb dropped near him but it didn't hurt him. Florence, her husband, and their six children would all kneel and pray. Such faith they had.

Every night in the seminary school we were shelled by the navy and every day we were bombed by the air force. One day, my brother Howard saw a fixed wing aircraft flying low over the school. When it reached the school's oval, a man dropped a small bomb out of the plane's window. The pilot appeared to have waited until he reached the oval to drop the bomb, so no one would be hit.

My father was living in Rangoon while we were in Insein. Every day he would go to the British embassy and kick up a row to evacuate his children from Insein to Rangoon. Finally, the British, Indian, and Pakistani embassies negotiated to evacuate civilians from Insein after the Burmese and the Karens signed a truce for one hour.

While my family was preparing to evacuate, I snuck out to the front line without their knowledge. I knew they would never have let me go. I wanted to fight, I wanted to be a soldier, and I wanted adventure.

One of the Karen soldiers gave me a gun and I went to the front line with my coworkers, shooting at the enemy in the distance as we went. A few hours later I returned to the seminary to look for my family. They were all gone. They had been evacuated to Rangoon by the foreign embassies. Even if they had still been there, I would have shown my face, and later quietly slipped away.

That was the day I joined the battle of Insein and the Karen Revolution. I was eighteen years old. I had made up my mind that I would stay until I died or could no longer fight. I was there at the very beginning of the revolution, in that first life-changing battle, and I stayed for the next five decades.

When I became a soldier, I was completely cut off from my family. I didn't dare contact Baby either, to tell her what had happened. A number of my relatives were teachers at the seminary school, but I couldn't contact them during the battle. It is difficult and dangerous to contact your family when you revolt. If the enemy had known who my relatives were, they would have taken action against them. My family might have been used as a means of persuading me to surrender. I needed to protect them. I decided not to have any contact with my family until we had achieved victory and the war was over. Only then would I find my family. But sometimes I missed them.

Infantry Warfare

The KNDO forces had previously attacked Mingaladon Airport in Rangoon and captured a lot of small arms from the arsenal there, including 20 millimeter Hispano Oerlikons, .5 heavy machine guns and .303 Browning machine guns. All the machine guns were removed from three stationary Spitfires. The Spitfires and two British twenty-five pounders were captured but left behind intact, as the Karens planned to use them later when they attacked Rangoon. Some of the airport's ground staff and crew members joined us. The KNDO set up the arsenal in the railway workshop where I had worked and recalled my former coworkers.

They managed to repair the damaged weapons. They repaired a Japanese eighteen pounder, a Japanese field artillery gun, and high explosive shells.

I was more interested in combat, so I continued fighting. I was attached to a group of deserters from the Burmese air force fighting in Insein. I had little experience in infantry warfare, but I found it to be very interesting. During this time I became a lance corporal and replaced a sergeant who had been killed.

By the seventh day of the battle, lines of communication were set up and the head teacher and students of the local seminary school organized cooking for the defenders. We totaled over one thousand men, five hundred of whom were permanent front line troops. To ensure food supplies, the rice mills were quickly taken from the Burmese Territorial Forces. They provided the Karens not only with rice but also with beans, which were made into curries. The meals were prepared and packaged using newspapers from the government printing press in the jail.

Ammunition supplies became a problem. Fortunately, old munitions were found buried beneath the grounds of the jail. The Japanese had used the Insein jail as their headquarters before their retreat. A number of chemists and volunteers were able to recycle the old munitions.

There were women soldiers at Insein. Some were attached to mortars and artillery and some were drivers. Others cooked rice and sent rice packages to the front line in vehicles driven by women. Everyone was involved in the fighting.

As the siege continued, Britain, India, and Pakistan attempted to broker negotiations to end the impasse. A delegation of diplomats led by the Anglican bishop of Rangoon, George West, arrived in Insein to conduct peace talks between Saw Ba U Gyi, the Karen bishop Francis Ah Mya, Prime Minister U Nu, and General Ne Win. As a result of the talks, Saw Ba U Gyi signed an agreement on April 6, 1949, that promised amnesty to Karen troops and allowed Karen civilians to keep weapons for their own protection.

There was a three-day ceasefire at the Insein front line while the talks were taking place. Some Burmese soldiers came without arms to visit our troops. Likewise, some of our soldiers also visited the Burmese troops without arms. We all knew each other from before the battle. Some of our soldiers had deserted from the Burmese army, navy, and air force. Others had deserted from various armed units such as the Union Military Police.

Our soldiers visited the Burmese by day and returned in the evening. They were even allowed to go to the cinema in Rangoon and come back in army trucks. They brought back fried noodles, drinks, and cigarettes. I didn't go with them because the war was not over yet. The Burmese were still our enemy and you can't be friends with your enemy.

During the ceasefire, our unit was posted with a platoon of the First Karen Rifles at a rice mill on the Hlaing riverbank. The Burmese navy gunboats were anchored at the mouth of the Twante canal, which flowed into the Hlaing River. Small river patrol UB boats and double-decker boats came slowly right up to Kasin village, opposite the bank of the rice mill. There they deployed more fresh troops and took new positions. As they came along for each trip, they announced in Karen with loud speakers, "Children of *Htawmeipa*. Do not shoot!"[3]

They repeated this over and over until they went away. We were told not to shoot at the boats unless we were shot at even though the boats were bringing reinforcements. Insein was located at a bend in the river. The boats were then able to surround the town during the ceasefire and prepare for battle. Beyond the river, in the villages, were the communists. It was difficult to recognize them because they didn't wear uniforms. You only knew they were there when they fired their guns.

On the third day, the peace talks failed, and our leaders came back from Rangoon. The fighting started all over again. The navy gunboats and the fresh troops from the opposite riverbank opened fire on us. All other fronts also opened fire. They bombarded us with naval guns, field artillery, mortars, and air raid assaults. The fighting was so intense, you could be killed at any time.

When some of our soldiers who had gone to Rangoon on the third day of the talks came out of the cinema, they had no idea that the ceasefire was over. They were told to get into the lock-up truck and were taken to the Rangoon central jail where they were put behind bars for three years.

One of those soldiers was from Tawwi village, near Nyaunglebin. He had been out in his field near the Rangoon-Mandalay highway one day tending his cattle. When he came home for lunch, his wife told him there were no vegetables. So he went back to pick some and encountered a convoy of Karen army trucks from Taungoo with reinforcements for Insein. Some of them knew him, so they persuaded him to go along with them. They had a spare Japanese machine gun with no one to handle it. He hesitated at first; then he agreed. This was how he joined the revolution. Even now, when someone takes too long to do something, we say, "Is he plucking vegetables?" Later, he was one of the men who went to the cinema when the ceasefire ended, so he became one of those locked up in the Rangoon central jail for three years. He had asked me for advice about whether he should go to Rangoon or not, and I had told him he had to make up his own mind.

It was a tough time in Insein. The enemy surrounded us in a crescent, so there was no coming and going. Fresh troops came in periodically to replace the deserters, who would go back to the villages. We had only salt and rice to eat every day. When the new reinforcements came, they brought food we could enjoy. If nobody came, we continued with rice and salt. Similarly, information only came with new people.

---

3. One of the ancient Karen leaders was known as Htawmeipa.

We lived a hard life during the battle. If you were in a trench you couldn't move, even to go to the toilet, because of the bombardment. When the beans from the rice mills had all been eaten, some people started eating cats and dogs, which we nicknamed "Italian goat." We used to go to the train station and pick up cigar and cigarette butts. We'd squash and roll them with paper and then smoke them. I remember the British and Japanese prisoners of war did the same thing. It doesn't matter if you are scared; you still have to go through the hardship.

Day by day our front line was getting narrower and narrower. We had to control our fire; our ammunition was running out. We only had five rifle rounds each and two full Bren gun magazines. We had to be smart about how we used our ammunition. We waited to shoot until the enemy was close so we wouldn't miss and waste a round.

While I was working in the railway workshop I had come to realize the power of carrying a gun. Those Burmese workers who had guns were able to push other workers around. I wanted to be in combat because I would have a gun. I thought that if I had a gun, no one would be able to push me around anymore. Yet I found that if I had a gun I was obliged to fight and not go to Rangoon to escape from it all.

I knew how to use a gun because the British left many guns behind after the Second World War. Villagers would pick them up and use them for hunting. When the British came back after the war to collect their weapons we had used up all their ammunition.

I had had no training as a soldier. My training was on the battlefield. My duty was to shoot the enemy and their duty was to shoot me. There was no room for feelings about my fellow man. Only God could decide who should live or die.

I saw many of my friends die. There was a university student with whom I was very friendly. Every day we would go to the front line together. One day my friend was riding on a jeep armed with weapons from the Spitfires captured at Mingaladon Airport when the Burmese fired on it. He was shot and killed. I felt sorry for him, but there were so many soldiers dying that after a while I couldn't feel sorry any more.

We built bunkers with rice bags on which we mounted an old Japanese machine gun. One day our men decided to test out the machine gun. Meanwhile, one of the other soldiers, my friend Po Ni, decided it was too noisy in the bunker so he took a stool outside the bunker and began reading a novel. He was warned about the machine gun but he said he wasn't worried. He was whistling as he was reading. As the machine gun started a bullet hit Po Ni. We looked outside and the book had fallen. We put him on the jeep and took him to the hospital.

Later we returned to see how he was and found him moaning loudly, with froth coming out of his mouth, when suddenly he went quiet. The doctor pronounced him dead, and told us to take him to the mortuary and return the next day for the funeral. When we came back the next day he was gone—and the nurses told us he'd been moved to the ward. Earlier in the mortuary two nurses began to wash and prepare him for his funeral when suddenly he began to cry out and scream. People rushed in to see what the matter was and found him alive. Later he told them that he had been so weak he couldn't make a noise, so they thought he was dead. He had heard the doctor say he was dead, but he was unable to tell them he was still alive. For a long time afterwards, he was very angry with that doctor. He wondered what sort of doctor he was if he couldn't tell if a person was alive or dead!

I was wounded twice in Insein. The first time, we were on a little hill, and the enemy was advancing. My gun stopped firing after one or two hours. The enemy hid behind a tree and began shooting. A gunshot hit my gun between the bolt and magazine. If it weren't for my rifle the bullet would have hit my face and neck. Another time, I was in a trench firing a Bren gun, and a Gurkha soldier with the Burmese army crawled along the ground toward us. He threw a hand grenade, but it didn't quite reach us. He threw another six or seven grenades on top of my trench, and I got a grenade splinter lodged in my head. Luckily, I had a steel helmet on because I was hit on the back of the head. They took me to the hospital and showed me the splinter. It was as small as a grain of rice. It was very painful, and I told the nurse, "If I had known it was so small, I would have stayed in the trench. I thought it was a big splinter!"

One night I stopped at a friend's house. There was an old Karen man there, sleeping at the same house. I had seen him before, but I didn't know him. Whenever the old man woke up he would pray. He prayed to God about five or six times that night. I couldn't sleep. I thought he had malaria. In the morning, the house's owner told me that every night the old man would get angry and scold God. Every day he would go to the hospital and at night he would ask God to look after the soldiers and reprimand him for letting three or more soldiers die.

I thought there was something wrong with him, but there wasn't. People pray to God, but instead he made demands of God. I thought maybe I should tell him to scold God for not helping us with our aim against the enemy. Sometimes people would see him coming and would move away, almost as if an enemy shell were headed straight at them. He was a short man with a short temper.

I never regretted becoming a soldier rather than following a career as an engineer in the railway workshop. Sometimes I missed my fiancée, Baby. After she had finished her nurse's training and I had finished my engineering training, we had planned to settle down and get married. But the war broke out. If the revolution had never happened, I would have married Baby and become a boiler inspector and then a foreman. When I was an officer I used to tell my men that I had studied to work on locomotive boilers and had passed my exams, but now I only worked with a gun.

The Karen Rifles in Mandalay

Before the revolution started, there were three Karen battalions in the Burma National Army: the First Karen Rifles were stationed at Taungoo in central Burma, the Second Karen Rifles at Prome (Pyay), and the Third Karen Rifles at Mandalay. When the revolution started, the Second and First Karen Rifles deserted the Burma National Army. The Third Karen Rifles were in Mandalay, too far from the other Karens to know what was happening, so the whole battalion was disarmed before they could defect.

The First Kachin Rifles were at Pyinmana.[4] They were ordered to reoccupy Taungoo. The Kachins arrived in Taungoo and sent a messenger to contact the Karens there who had deserted the Burma National Army. They wanted to negotiate. The Kachins told them that they had been ordered to attack and reoccupy Taungoo but had decided not to since we are all ethnic nationalities. But then the Kachins didn't know what to do. The Karens told them that they should try to help reinforce Insein and then occupy Rangoon.

The Kachins, however, told us that instead of going to Rangoon, they'd rather go to Meiktila and Maymyo and then from there to Mandalay, where they would release the whole captured battalion of Karen Rifles.[5] Then they would have one more battalion with which they could come back and occupy Rangoon. So they changed their direction. Instead of going to Insein, they went to Meiktila. The Kachins stayed in contact with the Burmese army. The Kachin captain Naw Seng contacted the other Kachins who had stayed neutral and didn't fight against or with the Karens.[6] From Taungoo they went to Meiktila on two trains. In the train they found all sorts of rations and ammunitions, medical supplies and reinforcements.

The Burmese had told the Kachins that some high-ranking officers were coming to Meiktila by plane. The Karens took one platoon of Karen soldiers and one

---

4. Pyinmana is a town close to Naypyidaw, Burma's capital since 2005. During the Second World War Pyinmana was a base of the Burmese Independence Army and it has symbolic importance for the national armed forces. It is considered the place in which Aung San and the Burmese army first turned against the Japanese and joined the allies, liberating Burma from the colonial era (Aung-Thwin and Aung-Thwin 2012).

5. Maymyo is a town located in Mandalay Region. The town was named by the British after a British colonel, Colonel May, and was later renamed by the military government of Burma as Pyin Oo Lwin. The town began as a military outpost and is currently home to the Defense Services Academy and the Defense Services Technological Academy, flagship institutions for Burma's armed forces.

6. Naw Seng was a decorated Second World War Kachin veteran. As commander of the First Kachin Rifles, he fought for the central government against the Burmese communists. He was later ordered to conduct operations against the rebel Karens, but he defected and joined the Karens in launching campaigns against the government. In late 1949, he organized the Pawng Yawng rebellion, a short-lived Kachin rebellion, before taking refuge in China. He later emerged again as military head of the CPB's North East Command in the late 1960s.

platoon of Kachin soldiers and quickly occupied the airport at Meiktila. The Karens and Kachins waited at the airport. When the two planes landed and the engine stopped, the leaders came down from the plane. The British pilots and the Burmese officers didn't know what was happening. Only when everyone got down from the plane were they asked to surrender. They were shocked by what had happened. There were about six or seven Burmese army jeeps that came to meet them. When the jeeps arrived they too were disarmed.

The British pilots asked for permission to go back, since their mission had been to Meiktila only. The Karens and Kachins refused and said that they would use the plane to go to Mandalay as it would be quicker than driving. The Burmese army in Mandalay didn't yet know what had happened in Meiktila. If the Karens and Kachins had gone to Mandalay in the jeeps, it would have taken a long time and the Burmese army may have found out what was happening in the meantime, so traveling by plane was the better option. The Karens told the pilots to forget about their mission and to only think about the present situation right now.

The platoon of Karen Rifles and Kachin Rifles took the two planes and landed in Mandalay headquarters. They disarmed the people that came to meet the plane and then they went straight to the Mandalay palace, the old Burmese king's palace where the interned Karen Rifles were being held. Some were drunk. They had no work so they only gambled and drank. The arriving platoons of Karen and Kachin Rifles told to them to hurry to the rifle court and arm themselves.

They were surprised seeing the Karen Rifles in uniform and some said that they heard the Karen Rifles had gone underground. The liberators told them that this was true and that they too would now be going underground. They armed the whole battalion and left. My boss, General Tamlar Baw, was in the First Karen Rifles and told me the story of what happened.[7]

Withdrawal from Insein

One month before our withdrawal, we were in Insein, with the enemy at the edge of the town and the river behind us. The enemy formed a crescent around us. They were even on the other bank of the river. When the enemy from the east bank of the river fired, some of their bullets reached their own men on the west side. Similarly, when the north and south fired, it reached their other men. We were in the center

---

7. General Tamlar Baw was a Karen revolutionary who began his military career as a British Army intelligence officer in preindependence Burma. In the Karen community today, he is known for his unwavering commitment to Karens' political aspiration for self-determination.

and bullets were flying around us in all directions. None of us bothered to dwell in trenches anymore as there was danger everywhere. We went out walking or by jeep. If your roll is not called, you're quite safe. We believed this even though we did not know what would happen from minute to minute and to whom. Whether the weather was wet or fine, we were still happy, with high morale and a belief that we were fighting for the rights of our people and for freedom and justice.

The Karen army was ordered by the KNU leaders to leave once they were surrounded. The withdrawal orders were to take effect starting May 21, 1949. After May 23, everyone who had not retreated would end up in the Insein central jail. There were several hundred Karen soldiers left. Some soldiers had already withdrawn because of the dangers, while others had stayed, wanting to fight. Most soldiers, though, were happy to leave the battle because after 111 days we had all had enough of fighting. We were glad to have survived. As they say, "you do or die." Our morale was still high and we felt we were fighting for something worthwhile. We knew that the Karens were being oppressed by the Burmese government. Things had escalated step by step after independence and we now knew we had to defend ourselves and our people. That's why the army was called the Karen National Defence Organisation.

The president of the Karen National Union, Saw Ba U Gyi, was with us at Insein. I remember that he encouraged us. He wasn't the operational commander, but he stayed with us until we all withdrew. The highest-ranking officer usually leaves first and the soldiers last, but he left last so as to give everyone confidence. He was easy to talk to and he was friendly with everybody. He would show interest in you and ask how you were feeling. Were you feeling happy? As a leader he gave the troops moral support, so that the soldiers would think that if even the president stays here, they could also.

On May 21, a section from our unit went to a tributary of the Hlaing River near the rice mill. In the daytime, we gathered planks to make rafts to secretly withdraw at night. At midnight we moved to the riverbank and found nothing. Some other people had stolen our rafts! On May 22, we again built rafts and again they were stolen. May 23 was the final and last day for us to withdraw and the same thing occurred. It seemed that the only thing left for us to do was to try to penetrate through the enemy lines at Danyingon. That night, I spoke to our men: "If we fight our way through, about half of us will survive with additional casualties. So, what shall we do? Shall we go back to Insein and make rafts again and cross the river in broad daylight?" Nobody answered. We rested in the dark. Everybody was quiet. We were all tired of thinking up ways to survive.

Hours later, a soldier came in a hurry and whispered that he could see an object like a boat coming along in the starlight. We all looked for the object. Sure enough, it was a boat. We pleaded with the boat's occupants to ferry us across.

Then we all stood up in a long line, and they came to the riverbank and ferried us across the river. At last! We had managed to cross the most difficult obstacle.

We proceeded on our journey to Sabyusu, past a communist held village and an enemy post at Kasin village on the same riverbank. While we were circumventing this village, five people came toward us, including two women. They invited us to take our meal with them and rest. We hesitated at first, because not long ago our Karen soldiers had been fighting the communists for the government. A soldier whispered in Burmese, "Wa wa sar, wa wa thay," which means "Eat your full, die with a full stomach." We laughed at him and followed those who came and invited us because they understood the saying, "the enemy of my enemy is my friend." We entered village after village and were greeted with smiles. They gave us rice and curry to eat and lots of other good food. After we had a good feed, they told us that they had been entertaining everybody who withdrew from Insein who came their way.

That day we finally got to Sabyusu. We could not proceed to Paet Kho because both villages were crowded and there wasn't sufficient water. The houses were full of people. Soldiers retreating from Insein were under houses, under trees, and on the ground. One of my close friends was Saw Wilbur, a student from Rangoon University. He and I set up our ground sheets and mosquito nets outside the village in the sun and rested under the nets for two days.

Throughout the Battle of Insein, I remained with the same unit. I had been a soldier, a lance corporal, and a corporal. Now we were at platoon strength and I became the platoon sergeant. I had twenty-seven men under my command and I was only nineteen years old. Even though I was younger than my soldiers, they still obeyed me.

On May 23, Insein town was empty and a white flag was hoisted at the jail. The enemy hesitated for three days thinking it was a trap and then later entered Insein. Insein had been the first major battle of the Karen Revolution.

4

WALKING ACROSS BURMA

After two months we were healthy and ready to move again. The villagers wanted us to stay longer and protect them from the Burmese soldiers. These people had suffered before at the hands of soldiers during the Japanese occupation, and we were worried that there might be reprisals if the Burmese army found these people helping us. If even one Karen soldier was found, there would be trouble.

We had a meeting about our destinations. Soldiers were told to join new units heading in the direction they wanted to go. I decided to join the troops going to Taungoo because I wanted to visit Peinzalok, where I had lived with my parents and siblings before the civil war started. The commander of my new unit was the brother of my friend Saw Wilbur. We had to part with our platoon.

There was a railway and a main road to Taungoo, but the Burmese occupied both. To reach the Karen headquarters we had to go on foot through the Pegu Yomas, a long mountain range in central Burma. The mountains gave us much more cover from the enemy than the plains, and we would pass with a local civilian escort through communist territory onto Karen-administered land.

Our new unit was varied. There were many soldiers from other units, including Captain Laurie and Captain Ba Thin. We were also joined by four women in their twenties—two telephone operators from the Mingaladon telephone exchange and two sisters who were both students of Judson College, Rangoon. They were stuck and couldn't take the train home so they had to walk with us.

We set off to Pokthinnyo, the last village at the foot of the Pegu Yomas, where we camped. The next day our civilian guides told us it was a treacherous journey and that we should carry a two-day ration of rice and also help carry some of the

44

women's belongings, as we could come across wildlife such as tigers or snakes—or the enemy itself. Some soldiers were superstitious and believed they would lose their innate male "power" if they touched a woman's belongings, but two soldiers (one a sergeant) and I felt sorry for the women and offered to carry some of their possessions until we got to Taungoo.

At dawn we set off, beginning our climb over the hills. By afternoon, the three of us who volunteered to carry extra loads were really tired. It seemed our backpacks were getting heavier each hour, but we dared not complain. When it was dark, we took off our packs and set up camp. It had been raining all day. We cut some bamboo to pitch a tent for four of us: the two sisters, the sergeant, and me. The tent was a foot from the ground. A fireplace was made between the sisters on one side and us two sergeants on the other side. We made a flattened bamboo floor and a bamboo roof covered with wild banana leaves. We built a big fire to cook rice. We were told to put the washed rice into lengths of bamboo with water one inch above the rice, to close the lid tight with bamboo leaves, and to place it close to the fire, leaning it on a bamboo line to boil. Then we reduced the fire to let the rice steam on the hot ashes. We used to cook fish, crabs, wild fowl, mushrooms, and other vegetables from the jungle in the same way.

I, like many of the other solders, had no previous experience with this method of cooking. If the lid is too tight, the bamboo explodes, and your meal drops into the fire, leaving an empty, cracked piece of bamboo. If the lid is too loose, it spills out all the rice and water. Correct adjustment of the fire is also important. That night I cooked the rice twice. The first time it exploded. The second time it disgorged its contents into the fire. That night the four of us had no rice to eat, so we shared the tin of condensed milk I found in my pack and drank water from the stream. Throughout the night our stomachs were in turmoil and we ran often to the toilet. Impure water and milk had not made a very good supper for us.

A few days earlier our guide had helped a group of three hundred troops from Thaton who had camped at the same spot. He told us that one of the soldiers was terrified of tigers so took great pains to be safe. He pitched his tent in the center of the camp and slept surrounded by a group of soldiers. In the middle of the night, a soldier coming back from the toilet screamed at the top of his lungs: he had just seen a tiger dragging away a corpse—the very soldier who was so scared of tigers! The whole camp was alerted and started firing their guns into the air to scare the tiger away. After we heard this story we couldn't sleep.

The next day we had to go around borrowing rice from others. The women asked us to cut a length of bamboo for them and they cooked the rice perfectly. We had forgotten that they were from the mountain areas, from Paleikkhi village, between Taungoo and Mawchi mine, so they knew how to survive in the wild. We only thought of them as Judson College students.

We set off on our trip in the pouring rain and stopped when we got to the last village on the Pegu Yomas. The next day we started our downhill journey, but we were still going uphill and downhill until we got to the Pegu River near Hpoung-gyi. All of us had to ford the river, and soldiers who were expert swimmers had to carry everyone's belongings across. We continued our journey to Kyundeik village, at the foot of the Pegu Yomas, but we didn't stop as we wanted to get to Shwe Aingdon village, where we had relatives, friends, and schoolmates.

When we finally got there, we were so happy and excited to see our friends. From the time we arrived, we started exchanging our revolutionary experiences and our combat stories. It was hours past midnight before we finally stopped talking. The next day our friends and relatives invited us to stay longer but after our morning meal, we continued on our journey. The next village, Sitbogyi, was just a mile away from Shwe Aingdon. As soon as we arrived, the villagers prepared food for us. We weren't hungry at all but they forced us to eat at least something. Karen villagers have a custom of hospitality; they must feed any visitor who comes to their home; no one must go hungry. If some troops come to their village, they slaughter and cook pigs or cattle. The villagers heard that we had served in the Battle of Insein, which had already become famous because it was the beginning of the revolution and it was a fierce and critical battle that could have gone either way. They heard that we had been eating only salt and rice, sometimes starving for weeks, so they piled our plates with rice and curry.

In the afternoon we got to Daik-U Railway Station and boarded a special troop train to Nyaunglebin. There we met Tabu, my cousin on my mother's side, and some friends. Like many of the Karen youth, he automatically became part of the Karen Revolution and was stationed in the local brigade.

The next day we continued our journey by train to Kanyuntkwin, arriving in the afternoon, and were immediately invited to dinner at the Chinese school. We couldn't believe our eyes at all the dishes we were served, after having starved during the Battle of Insein. The Chinese really know how to cook. From the time we got over the Pegu Yomas, we'd been having feast after feast. It was an unusual pleasure for us.

We camped at Kanyuntkwin and early the morning we set out on foot for Pyu. Two bullock carts carried our belongings, but we carried our own guns and equipment. We found it hard going, as we were not used to the physical exercise of climbing hills and walking long distances. The communists also kept blowing up Burmese bridges at places where we wanted to cross, like between Kanyuntk-win and Pyu. Arriving at Pyu at noon, we were tired, hungry, and feeling very hot. We were put up in the civil hospital building at the edge of the town and told to take our meals at the mess in the center of town.

Our battalion commander, Colonel Richmond, was invited out for dinner at the Zayatwaddy sugar factory, so he left some money with Po Ni, the soldier who was seriously wounded at Insein. The colonel said that if we were very hungry but our food at the mess was not ready, Po Ni should take us out to eat. Po Ni, however, just asked us if we wanted to follow him as he was going out to eat at the Chinese shop. Nobody followed him, thinking that he was joking. After all, where could he get money at a time like this?

When the food was ready at the mess, the quartermaster told a signalman to inform us. He didn't even get halfway to us before he returned to the quartermaster and told him that the men wouldn't come because their stomachs were full. The quartermaster had sent a man who obviously had a screw loose, so we were starved all day long.

By dark all of us were very hungry—and angry, with both Colonel Richmond and the quartermaster. We started firing our guns into the air. People thought the communists had attacked us so they phoned Colonel Richmond, who rushed back from the dinner party in a jeep with an armored personnel carrier escort. We all took position to fight him. He got down from his jeep and walked toward us unarmed so nobody would shoot him. We controlled our tempers and settled the problem. It wasn't the fault of either Colonel Richmond or the quartermaster. It was the two other idiots that had caused the whole thing. Po Ni told us calmly that since nobody followed him to eat at the shop, he spent the money on food and drinks and gambled the rest away.

The quartermaster brought us pots and pans, rations, and a cow, saying that nobody dared cook for us anymore. But why should we cook for ourselves, we thought, and we demanded cooked food as the other unit had been given. So they cooked for us and gave us drinks and smokes. Later on, I thought that maybe we should have just complained, rather than kicking up a row.

The next morning, we set off early on foot. Another bridge had been blown up by the communists between Pyu and Bambwaygon. In the afternoon we caught the train from Bambwaygon to Taungoo. When we saw the distant lights of Taungoo in the evening, we had a strange feeling in our hearts. We recalled the days before the war broke out. Arriving at Taungoo felt like peace. The soldiers and the Kachin and Karen military police were well dressed just like they had been during British rule. We were so excited to see them.

The next day we reported to the War Office and were assigned to special duty with Colonel Richmond, who was a battalion commander in the Karenni Brigade known as the Taungoo troops. He was from Taungoo and had been with us when we withdrew from Insein. At first I liked him, but when we got to Taungoo there was a lot of alcohol available, and his soldiers started misbehaving.

The units were called by the place they came from or by the commanding officer's last name. My unit had soldiers from all different backgrounds, deserters from the Burmese air force, navy, artillery corps, and the railway workshop. We couldn't be called by the place we came from so my unit had no name. When my unit joined with Colonel Richmond's we became Richmond's Unit.

We stayed in Taungoo for a fortnight before we left for special duty in Taung-gyi (in Shan State) where we joined the First Kachin Rifles who had deserted the Burmese army. When we joined the Kachins, Colonel Richmond asked us all to get tattoos. The Shan believe if you have a tattoo the enemy cannot shoot you, so they would cover themselves with Shan letters. I didn't want to be tattooed, as I thought it was a bit of nonsense, but they insisted. I couldn't think of anything to tattoo, so I just wrote "Love." They said it was too little; I exclaimed, "No. Love rules the world!" Then I saw the words "Love is blind" on an embroidery, so I asked to have that tattooed on my right shoulder. I was going to have the same tattooed on my left shoulder, but as they were tattooing, I remembered the saying "God is Love"; to say that "Love is blind" would mean that God is blind, which wasn't right, so I asked them to stop. So, on my left shoulder there is only the word "Love" in capital letters.

We planned to go to Taunggyi via Mawchi Mine, Hpasawng, and Loikaw in Karenni State; we all got into an army truck, with Colonel Richmond in a jeep, and later camped at Istu suburb, on the east bank of the Sittang River. On arrival at Taunggyi, we first went to meet with the elders, all of us in uniform and fully equipped. Then, we put one soldier in each house if the houses were close to each other; otherwise we had two soldiers to a house. Our task was to safeguard the Karens in Taunggyi in case of emergency, but we were on reconnaissance duty, so we dressed as civilians for this task and kept our weapons concealed.

Every five days people came from the outskirts and surrounding areas to a market. The day after we arrived was market day, so the people I was assigned to protect asked me to accompany them to it. I was nervous at first because we were on special duty and supposed to be undercover. But they told me that as I had never been to Taunggyi before, nobody would know me, so there would be no problem. I thought the same and I followed them to the bazaar where all the different races wore their colorful costumes and I saw tribes I had never seen before.

While I went around looking through the bazaar, suddenly I came across a policeman. We stared at each other. He looked familiar. When he got close, both of us smiled. We had met when we were patients in Rangoon General Hospital. We greeted each other and had a brief chat. He had no idea that I had joined the Karen Revolution.

One Sunday at church, I met Pastor John Thet Kyi, who had known me since I was a child. I also met Charlie Alexander, whose father was from Kangalay and who was apparently related to me. From then on, I hardly went out. People were identifying me, one after another!

We had been in Taunggyi for a month doing reconnaissance when all of a sudden we were recalled to Loikaw. On arrival at Loikaw we were located on the

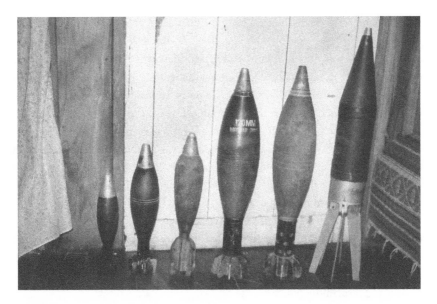

FIGURE 3.   Artillery display in Manerplaw

west bank of the Balu Chaung (the source flowed from Inlay Lake). The next day, August 12, 1949, we moved back to Taunggyi, this time with a convoy of two hundred trucks and jeeps. On the way, at Hopong, we came to a brief halt; it was getting dark, and all the vehicle lights were lit. Suddenly we saw flares in the air, about two miles ahead of us, then two truckloads of the Thirteenth Union Military Police (UMP) came out of Taunggyi to ambush our column.[1] When we advanced a little further, the UMP started firing more flares, including small arms and mortars, but then quickly retreated.

In June 1949 the Karen war establishment introduced major changes to the structure of our forces. The army, which had been part of the Karen National Defence Organisation, was renamed the Kawthoolei Armed Forces (KAF) and its war office was located in Papun. The name was changed to show that the army was part of Karen territory. As today, many KNDO units were essentially local security forces and they were not interested in going elsewhere in the country to fight. When we have achieved victory, our Karen homeland will be called Kawthoolei, or

---

1. The Union Military Police was a paramilitary force created by the U Nu government in 1948. Like the Karen Rifles in the army, some Karen UMP forces defected when the Karen rebellion began (Smith 1999). After General Ne Win took power in 1962, the UMP was absorbed into the army (Selth 2002; Callahan 2003).

peaceful land.[2] Although deserters from the Burmese forces still considered themselves air force, navy, or army, they also took on the KAF name so that we were all the same. It was now more of a Karen national armed force than before, and evolved into the present-day Karen National Liberation Army (KNLA). Only the Delta Command of the KNU and KNDOs in the Irrawaddy Delta region did not unify with the others, because they were cut off by the Burmese military forces.

Previously, units had been named after locations or given the commander's name. However, it was decided that if the unit was named after the location, it might discourage soldiers from leaving that area. If the unit was named after a commander, it gave the message that it was the commander's personal unit. So, units were only given numbers.

Our column arrived back in Taunggyi on August 13, 1949. Our plan was for the Karen, Kachin, Karenni, and Pa-O troops to combine forces and occupy Taunggyi without firing a single round. The Karens and Kachins were to surround the UMP headquarters and disarm them, and a unit was to go to the police station and disarm the police.

My task was to go to the Burmese battalion commander's residence and capture him alive. We surrounded his residence and I went behind his house. As I arrived, he jumped down and ran. I told him to stop, but he continued running. We were ordered not to shoot unless shot at first, so he escaped. We captured his captain adjutant in his house. We were on our way to the treasury when we came across the battalion commander's jeep at a cross road; he challenged us and asked us who we were. As we dismounted from the truck, he tried to escape in his jeep, so we fired three warning shots. We told him to stop, but he didn't, so we fired more shots. One bullet hit the batman who was driving the jeep on the head; another hit the battalion commander on the thigh. He stayed in the jeep and we continued to our next target, the treasury. There was a section of the UMP guarding the treasury. We disarmed them and took over. One of their battalion commanders tried to run out the back doorway. I was carrying a Bren gun, which was difficult to handle. But I couldn't shoot anyway unless we were shot at.

The whole town was now occupied, but it was night, and no one knew who was who, so we told everyone to stay where they were. We left some of our men at the treasury office, where we captured two big transmitters, and advanced further to the police station that the Kachins had already taken. We came back to our men who we had left at the treasury. It was about seven o'clock in the morning

---

2. Kawthoolei has two territorial definitions. Its technical definition refers to the KNU-controlled area, which today is the narrow strip of land along the Thailand-Burma border. The other definition refers to the aspirational Karen country that includes the areas in Burma that Karens have historically inhabited.

as we passed a section of the Gurkha UMP.[3] They looked at us in surprise. A corporal came toward us, saluted me, and asked what they should do. They were not loyal to the Burmese. He asked me who we were, as there were also some Sikh troops with us who looked after the vehicles. Some mechanics asked whether the British troops had returned. I replied that we were Karens.

A soldier with the Burmese UMP also asked me who we were, and I told him not to point his gun at me and that I would tell him why later. In our unit we had a sergeant who had deserted from the same Burmese unit as this soldier, so I told the Karen soldier to go and get his gun in case the Burmese UMP soldier attacked us. We escorted those we disarmed to our Tactical Operation Command headquarters. They couldn't guess which troops we were; the Burmese armed forces had so many enemies that they didn't know which one was attacking them.

We found 27 *lakhs* of rupees stored in the treasury.[4] At that time one rupee equaled 16 annas and there were 64 pice in one rupee. You could buy fried noodles for two annas, so 27 *lakhs* of rupees was a lot of money. Moments later, the Karen authorities arrived, and we handed over all the captured things.

Six *lakhs* belonged to the Sawbwas, the Shan princes who were hereditary rulers in Shan State, so we returned it to them. The Shan Sawbwas were allies with the Karens and ordered their troops not to shoot the Karens, while the Karens ordered their soldiers not to shoot Shans. Some Shans helped the Karens occupy Taunggyi and were given the opportunity to join the Karen forces.

We sent the remaining 21 *lakhs* of rupees to Taungoo. The two big transmitters were moved to the Karen town of Papun in the hills to the south and used for broadcasting. We reported our activities, about the treasury and the two transmitters, to the Tactical Operation Command. Orders came for our unit to move to the civil supplies department and take over security for it. Within a couple of days, all the supplies were distributed and our unit had to take position at the Buddhist monastery at the edge of the town facing toward Inlay Lake and Nyaungshwe.

Our unit was stationed at Taunggyi for a month, then we had to move to Pantaing, between Loilem and Maing Pun. We carried out ambushes and skirmishes behind enemy lines, with a platoon of Gurkhas and one of local Pa-O, who were related to Karens attached to our unit. After another month, our unit was to report to the column headquarters at Taunggyi. The Kachin column headed by Captain Naw Seng moved to Kachin State, escorting civilians, including some Karens and

---

3. The Gurkha UMP was a police force made up of Gurkhas, a famous mercenary militia from Nepal. The majority of the Gurkhas came to Burma with the British administration during the colonial era and many remained in Burma after the British left.

4. A *lakh* is a unit of measurement common only in South Asian societies: one *lakh* equals a hundred thousand units.

a few others. Some of us briefly stayed in Loilem. At Namsan airport there were no Burmese soldiers. But we heard a plane was bringing Burmese soldiers, so we retreated back to rejoin our unit while the Burmese army occupied Loilem.

After resting for a fortnight, our unit was posted to Hsihseng between Taung-gyi and Loikaw. A couple of days later, we received orders that our unit was to be attached to Wungyi U Hla Pe.[5] There were two Hla Pes, one was a sergeant and the other had been a Pa-O member of the Burmese parliament and cabinet minister in U Nu's government who left to join the revolution. We had heard of Hla Pe the politician, but we assumed we were guarding the sergeant and couldn't understand why people were honoring this man wherever we went. Later on, Colonel Richmond asked about U Hla Pe the cabinet minister and we realized we had been protecting him the whole time!

There was a problem between Colonel Richmond and our unit regarding Christmas. We wanted to relax and celebrate Christmas in Taunggyi. He rejected our proposal, as he wanted us to celebrate in the Pa-O area (no man's land). We were angry as we packed up and got ready to move out of Hsiheng despite Colonel Richmond's orders. Wungyi U Hla Pe came to our unit in tears and beseeched us not to leave; the villagers also came and begged us, in tears. We were very friendly with the villagers and had defended them from enemy atrocities; we had compassion for them so we remained.

Colonel Richmond, however, had angered our unit again and again. We had no more patience with him. Finally, we left Shan State, Wungyi U Hla Pe, and the Pa-O people and headed toward Taunggyi. When we got to Hopong, which is a junction for Taunggyi and Loikaw, we were told that Taunggyi was now occupied by Burmese troops and that the Karen troops had withdrawn the day before. The Karens had occupied Taunggyi for between two and three months.

We went back to Hsihseng and were told our troops had withdrawn. It seemed every time we arrived somewhere we were told the Karen forces had already withdrawn. The next day we moved along the Hopong-Loikaw main road and in two days we arrived in Loikaw. Our unit reported to the First Karenni Brigade headquarters and was posted near the airstrip. Like the Pa-O, the Karenni people and the Karens are closely related.

Shortly afterwards, I was selected to undergo artillery training at Loikaw. Our commanding officer was an Anglo-Burmese called Captain Allan Bond. After training, our field gun detachment was deployed near Pekon, attached to the Tactical Operation Command, so when Karen troops attacked the Moe Byai area we had to give artillery cover. This was my first artillery operation. I liked doing

---

5. Wungyi is a Burmese term used for cabinet ministers.

all the calculations for firing weapons; it was not as tiring as infantry, where you face many physical obstacles. A few months later the enemy attacked the brigade headquarters for a couple of days and occupied it. Our artillery unit withdrew according to plan and was posted at Hpasawng.

There is a saying that "you can lose a hundred petals but not the stem of the flower." Our strategy was to win the war. We could lose a hundred battles but it didn't matter so long as we won the war. So when the Burmese reoccupied Taungoo in 1950, short-term morale was not an issue; we were in this for the long term. After sixty-seven years, the war is still going on and we still haven't lost.

LIFE AS A SOLDIER

One day in 1950 Bo San Gyaw and Major Billy were on their way from Hlaing-bwe to Mawchi Mine. They dropped in to visit overnight and told us about the Light Brigade. The brigade had obtained some artillery equipment, and didn't know how to use them, so they asked for an officer to go and organize the artillery unit. In 1950 I was promoted to a lieutenant and transferred to the Light Brigade headquarters at Hlaingbwe, near Hpa-An, in Karen State in southern Burma. I think the military hierarchy chose me because I had more education than others; I could read maps and do calculations for aiming the guns. It was handy knowledge to have.

There were two divisions in the eastern command where I was. The No. 1 Division commander was Major General Saw Bala Sein, and the No. 2 Division commander was Major General Saw Ta Ka Paw. The Light Brigade converted to the No. 4 Brigade, commanded by Brigadier Saw Elmo Peel. My unit converted from the Light Brigade Artillery to the No. 4 Brigade Artillery.

When I first arrived at the Light Battalion the artillery guns hadn't yet arrived, so I was attached to Htilon battalion, the A company. The company commander was Captain Pyi Thein. Major Billy was a battalion second-in-command at the advance headquarters. All three of us stayed together at Taung Galay (now Hpa-An airport), where we were once attacked by the enemy from Hpa-An, but they were beaten back by our troops to the other side of the river.

At Hlaingbwe we had five guns, two two-pounders and three eighteen-pounders, which the Japanese artillery had left them behind when they retreated. They were easier to drag by bullocks than the British guns. We found the shells the

Japanese had buried, too. All our artillery came from the Japanese; other weapons we captured from the Burmese army. We worked closely with the bullocks. Sometimes we had to dismantle the guns and transport them by boat, which was difficult as they were heavy.

I trained thirty soldiers to use the guns. The gun crew included ethnic Chin soldiers from western Burma and Gurkhas, the famed Nepalese mercenaries, but the majority in our unit was Karen. It was difficult because when the Japanese left their guns behind and buried them, they took the range finders with them. We dug them out, but it was much harder to aim without the range finder. We were at the Salween River and would fire one round, watch it drop in the water, and from that calculate the required elevation. We then used bamboo sticks to mark the height and map the distance to Hpa-An.

We had to pray that the shell would get there without an accident. Some soldiers suspected that I didn't want to fire at Hpa-An. They thought that there must be some people I knew there because the shell always fell into the river. When the Burmese gunboats came up the river, the shells always missed. Even if we wanted to hit them, we couldn't. Sometimes I would get angry and shout at them, saying that they should try shooting without a range finder!

After about a year we found a Japanese artillery officer who had stayed behind when the Japanese left Burma. He had hidden among the Karen, married a Karen woman, and had two or three children. He was quite fed up with war but was also afraid of us. I coaxed him to join the Karen Revolution and appointed him my second-in-command. When he saw the guns, he recognized them as the ones he used during the war and immediately saw that the problem was the lack of rangefinders. He ended up doing the same things as me, firing in the Salween River to work out the elevation necessary to hit the target. I said to the soldiers who had joked that I couldn't hit the targets that here was a real artillery officer who couldn't hit the target with these guns either!

On August 12, 1950, the KNU president Saw Ba U Gyi was assassinated in Hto Kaw Koo.[1] He had been attending the first KNU congress since fighting broke out in Papun and was traveling through the hills near Hlaingbwe. Saw Ba U Gyi and his party stopped at a hut beyond a stream where the elephant boys used to sleep.[2] Someone told the Burmese soldiers he was there, so they surrounded the

---

1. Saw Ba U Gyi's body was taken to Moulmein and put on public display. He was forty-five years old at the time. Today, August 12 is commemorated by Karens as Martyrs' Day. The following eight months would witness some of the heaviest fighting in the civil war while the KNU was without effective leadership (Smith 1999).

2. Elephant boys, also known as *mahouts*, were young men who were in charge of herding elephants.

hut and told him to surrender. He refused and was killed. Colonel Richmond was also assassinated around this time in Mae Sai near the Karenni border.

When we were on our mission in Hlaingbwe area, we had met General Ta Ka Paw and his guards. General Ta Ka Paw was a division commander. He was a good commander, and our unit combined with theirs. Sometimes we carried out our own guerrilla activities behind enemy lines, returning to his unit after each mission.

While we were away operating in the enemy area, General Ta Ka Paw was assassinated by Bo Win, a Karen from the No. 5 Brigade. Another general was jealous of Ta Ka Paw and asked Bo Win to assassinate him. Bo Win was Colonel Lin Htin's intelligence officer and would later surrender to the Burmese.

No one else was around when he was assassinated. We were all doing guerrilla warfare behind enemy lines. As soon as we received this information, we rushed back to the Hlaingbwe area immediately. We combined all his guards with our unit and went around the area. We recalled all deserters and recruited new recruits to increase our unit's strength

I was on the front line for two years at Hpa-An and around Moulmein. Hpa-An was important because we could pin the enemy down there. Otherwise they would disturb us at Hlaingbwe. It was a good place for tactical movements, and we kept moving around. I was looking after one battery of five guns with six gunners. Four detachments made one unit or battery.

We didn't have any rest time away from army life. When I was posted to Hlaingbwe, there was no church. If we wanted to attend church, we had to go to the Karen Christian villages about four to seven miles away. When we were successful in a movement or operation, whether it be attacking or defending, we lined up all the captured materials in a circle and thanked God for it. Later we became slack and proud. When we captured something there was no more thanking God for it. From then on, our situation did not progress so well.

One of the Burmese army strategies was to call a ceasefire and then use it as an opportunity to prepare for an attack. A ceasefire could also be a means for the Burmese to find out more about their enemies: for example, how the enemy's morale was and their location. In the end, we would be forced to surrender. Another ploy was to disarm us with assurances that we could remain along the Karen border as border guard forces, and since heavy weapons aren't needed in peacetime, we wouldn't be armed. And if we didn't like the idea, they could send their troops to be guards, but of course, with tanks and cannons. The Burmese would also ask if we hadn't suffered long enough.

The Burmese continue to implement these tactics today. Over the years, the Karens have found lots of minerals in Karen State. The Burmese said that if the minerals were mined by the Burmese state, it would be good for the economy and we could feed our families well and build big houses. The Burmese cut down a big teak tree that was hundreds of years old—a tree that six to seven people could circle holding hands— and promised to put it in a museum; instead, they sold the timber to the Chinese.

We believe that "right is might" and not "might is right." That way you have lots of supporters and no one can take anything from you. It is also important to do the right thing; then everyone will appreciate it and respect you. We say the Karen people are like water and the Karen army is like fish. If there is water the fish can survive; if there is no water the fish cannot survive. We don't want the water to be drained away. Enemy troops would drive Karens from their villages and they would run to Thailand with nothing. When the enemy troops came into Karen areas they ate all the food—pigs, cattle, chickens. They forced the people out, thus draining out the water. But we weren't reliant on villages for food. We were mobile and took food with us when we traveled.

We were never paid a salary; we depended on our knowledge and our sacrifices. As for the Burmese army, it depended on money. If Burmese soldiers were not paid, they did not fight. The Burmese army recruited, sometimes forcibly, many unemployed people in Burma who joined to support their families. They weren't fighting out of patriotism but to survive, for if they didn't get money, their families would starve. If there was no more money, there would be no more soldiers. The Karens raised money for their revolution through tax and customs duty at the border. When the Burmese people went to trade with Thailand, they went through Karen territory and we charged them a tax. The whole Karen state depended on that tax.

Because we didn't get paid, our families had to look after themselves by growing vegetables and raising livestock. We had some deserters from the Karen army because they realized the reality of what they were doing. The soldiers from the rural areas were mostly used to the difficulties of jungle life, but the soldiers from Rangoon who joined the revolution sometimes struggled as it was hard for them to either go back or stay on.

I never found it hard. I never wanted to give up because I knew what it would be like from the beginning. I knew there would be sacrifices and no pay and I still joined up. When recruits join the Karen army, they are interviewed about why they want to join. They usually all say they want to fight. They are told about the sacrifices and are asked from the beginning if they can withstand the hardships, but nobody says they won't join because of it.

The revolution was also like attending Karen language classes. Because I had learned Karen during the Japanese invasion, I could understand quicker than others, especially those from the Irrawaddy Delta region who only spoke Burmese. They found it difficult because they only spoke Burmese and the hill Karens didn't understand them even though all were Karen.

FIGURE 4.   Ralph (last row) with KNU comrades along Moei River

If we needed any money, we had to ask our wives. If my wife sold an animal—a chicken, a goat, a pig or a turkey—she would give me some money. We were given one uniform per year. We wore *longyis* every day and only wore our uniforms on special occasions.[3] We fought in our longyis but in combat we also wore shorts. We were taught that if we needed a gun, we had to quickly go and pick up the enemy's. If we attacked the enemy, we would take their uniforms, their guns, and their ammunition. We would wear the enemy uniforms. Karen women knew that Karen soldiers had no money. I had no money and my wife had no money, but the villagers helped.

In fifty years, I was never paid, even when I was a brigadier general. I was never paid after I left the war either. We couldn't work in Thailand because we were refugees and the immigration police might catch us. Instead the United Nations High Commissioner for Refugees (UNHCR) gave me a small allowance. In my whole career the only time I was paid was when I worked in the railway workshop when I was eighteen years old. My wife, Sheera, was never paid a salary either. Everyone made personal sacrifices for the sake of a better future for our children.

When I was with the artillery I slept in the bunker with the guns. When there was no fighting I could sleep at the advanced headquarters hut. I remember one

---

3. A *longyi* is a sarong-like traditional garment worn by both men and women.

night a soldier was on guard duty at an observation post. He was just standing there and smoking and thinking. When I went to check, I asked him what he was thinking about. He said, "It's just fighting, fighting, fighting. There's no one in my life to call me Daddy. Will it end with fighting, or will there ever be a chance for my children to call me Daddy?"

Sometimes I would think like that soldier. Would I one day live a normal life and settle down or would I die alone as a bachelor?

The Fall of Hlaingbwe

In April 1953, the enemy launched a massive joint military operation (involving the army, navy, and air force) on our liberated territory. The enemy started an artillery and mortar bombardment that lasted for three days. Naval gunboats bombarded from the Salween River and the air force bombed and strafed twice a day. I was with the antitank gun crew in the gun post during the operation. After two or three days of shelling, the tanks advanced.

On the fourth day the battle became fiercer. The enemy infantry and tanks confronted our frontline. The shell of the first shot we fired exploded in the chamber of our gun. After a few moments, when the smoke and dust cleared, I saw that our antitank gun was completely destroyed. All the gun crew in the bunker were wounded. My driver and I were standing behind them and the jeep was behind both of us. I felt a pain and I looked around my body and found no wound. I took off my shirt and asked the driver to look around; there were no signs of major injury but I had been wounded on my right thigh. Out of the six-gun crew, five were wounded, along with me. Only one gunner and my jeep driver were not hurt. The driver and I carried all of them onto the jeep and he drove. I think God saved the jeep driver to take us to the hospital.

The driver was going to take us to Nounglon Second Battalion hospital, because it was closer than Hlaingbwe. We could hear the sound of some enemy tanks heading toward Nounglon, behind the hill. The Second Battalion was adjacent to our front line. Only the Zwekabin cliff (Kwekabaw) stood between our two front lines. I told the driver to take us to Hlaingbwe instead, otherwise we and the enemy tanks would be entering Nounglon at the same time, and our wounded would not be able to run. At Kalauk Noe, our jeep got onto the Nounglon-Hlaingbwe road. When we got to Htilon we met Brigadier Elmo Peel. He asked us about the combat situation at the frontline. I told him briefly and continued on our journey to the Hlaingbwe hospital. The Third Battalion at Maekaraw was on our right flank and had to withdraw to Kamamaung. We had to withdraw from Hpa-An to the Kamahta area.

When we finally arrived at the hospital, Colonel Aung Din, a doctor, came to dress our wounds. He came to me first but I told him to dress the wounds of the others first because there were no painkillers or anesthetics. I said, "If they scream, I will scream also. If they are quiet, I will be quiet also." We were all half unconscious. I recall wanting the others to make some noise so that I could know if they were alive or not. One corporal next to my bed had shrapnel in his mouth, when it was his turn he didn't make a noise, his eyes just blinked. When it was my turn the doctor tried to find the shrapnel with his finger. I just whistled and sweated. I didn't want to scream.

While they were operating on our wounds, an enemy plane came and machine-gunned the surroundings. All the nurses and the doctor and other patients ran for shelter; only our gunners and I could not run. Bombardier Kaw Taik and I knew about the air raid, but the other gunners were unconscious and knew nothing. Fortunately, everyone survived the attack.

The same evening at dusk the hospital was evacuated to Ma eh village. I was admitted to the hospital for a week. I was then directed to go and stay at Dr. Aung Din's house at the Ka Maw Le Buddhist monastery, about one mile from the hospital. Dr. Aung Din's daughter was married to my brother-in-law Moses's younger brother, so we were all like family. Dr. Aung Din's house was more like a sanctuary for him and his family. The doctor was also Christian. It didn't matter that their house was in a Buddhist monastery compound. He and his family prayed Christian prayers while the monks chanted Buddhist prayers.

Dr. Aung Din had another beautiful daughter called Claris. Her nickname was Ah Pu. She was a beauty queen and had been Miss Moulmein. I had met her before while I was stationed in the Hlaingbwe area because her father was a full colonel in the revolution and the chief medical officer. Ah Pu took care of me while I recovered. She was training to be a nurse, so she dressed my wounds, rather than having a nurse come from the hospital. While I recovered and she cared for me, we fell in love.

We were in love, but we had no time to marry. I felt it was too early for me to get married, and we both wanted to concentrate on our work and duties. We thought the war would be over within a few months—or years—and then we could get married. But life didn't turn out that way. If the war had ended then, we may have gotten married.

When my sisters in Rangoon heard that I was engaged to Miss Moulmein, they were all overjoyed. They bought presents and sent them with the man who had told them the news. They were so happy to receive news like that about me, and always afraid they would instead receive news that I had been killed. But they were disappointed when they heard we didn't get married.

The last time I saw Ah Pu, she was working as a nurse. In the end she married a doctor from Rangoon General Hospital. In 2014 her younger brother came to a church conference in Perth. We were so happy to see each other, and everyone wanted to know how we were already such good friends. So I explained that we were together when we were young but we hadn't seen each other in sixty-five years, and that's why we were so happy. I didn't tell them that we almost became brothers-in-law.

When I was able to walk, I resumed duty at Hlaingbwe Pagoda Hill where my artillery unit was posted. We were on the hill and the enemy was just below the hill, about three hundred yards away. We occupied the hill and had the advantage. The enemy then began a whispering campaign to discredit us. Some people would make friends with our troops, bringing them liquor or smokes, and at the same time start whispering propaganda to demoralize our troops. The enemy also said that they wouldn't harm us if we surrendered, and some soldiers believed them. We stayed for three or four months on Pagoda Hill before we had to withdraw, so the enemy captured the hill.

To adapt to the new conflict landscape, the KAF strategic command changed the plan from conventional to guerrilla warfare. Our artillery unit moved to Thawaw Thaw and kept all the artillery pieces concealed. We only needed small arms. Otherwise we would be pinned down and couldn't move easily. If we used mobile warfare the enemy would find it hard to work out our intentions. They would also find it hard to bomb us from planes if we were moving around.

The next day our unit moved to Kwilay village, on the Hlaingbwe riverbank, and spent the night there. Early the next morning, at 4 a.m., everybody had to prepare to fight and take their positions. At about 8 a.m. the enemy's 108th Light Infantry Battalion attacked. The fighting lasted fifteen minutes before our troops dispersed. The majority of our troops crossed the river and retreated. About half an hour later, the firing ceased.

Sergeant Neh Kya Kho (with a Bren gun), Corporal San Kyi (with a rifle), and I (with a revolver and a rifle) met each other outside the village. The three of us were the last to leave the place. We were given verbal orders only to withdraw to Mae Ta Mu if we could not resist the enemy attack. None of us had any idea where Mae Ta Mu village was. The main reason for going there was to find out whether the enemy was holding the village or if they had retreated. So, once we found the village, we sneaked in to make sure of the exact situation.

When we got into the village, we saw the enemy and the porters busily ransacking every house. We opened fire and quickly got out of the village. There was a little stream, so we got into it and kept on firing for twenty minutes so that if there were any enemy fighting patrols around they would return to the village and we could move out easily.

The three of us managed to move out freely but none of us had any idea where to go because we were not familiar with the area. At that time we had no radio for communication. The runner system was the only way of communicating. We had to use our own common sense to contact each other.

We thought that Mae Ta Mu village was at the Thailand-Burma border, so we headed due east. After going around in circles for some time in the bush, we came across a hut and some villagers. We sneaked slowly toward them. Fortunately, some of them knew us and guided us to our own troops' position. About twenty minutes later we finally found our troops. Because we had gone around in circles, we took the whole day to go from Kwilay village to our troops' position when it was only three miles away. We thought we had gone far away from the enemy.

After the withdrawal from Hlaingbwe we stayed in Buddhist and animist villages. When people worship spirits, they slaughter and cook a pig and offer the pork and drinks to the evil spirits. Then the family, from the parents right down to the youngest child, gathers together, ties their wrists with white thread, and recites some words. After pacifying the spirits, the family and visitors are allowed to eat and drink together. I would enjoy myself and get drunk.

Before they prepared all these things, we had to take our guns and backpacks and go and stay in other houses and come back after their dealings to the evil spirits. They said that if there was a Bible in our bags or in the house, they could not call the evil spirits, because the evils spirits would never come near a Bible.

Before we got on to the convoy to go to battle, the chaplain would pray. We would sing hymns like Solid Rock in Karen the whole way. When they heard us, some ran away. Because the word hope in Karen is *yer ta mu la* but in Burmese this sounds like *ye tet moe la* which means, the water is rising, the rain is coming.

After Hlaingbwe fell we couldn't fight on a big scale anymore, we buried the guns just like the Japanese had. When the Burmese captured the gunners, they forced them to disclose where the guns were hidden.

Without artillery I was without a job. We stayed at the Mae Ta Mu front line and about a week later I was recalled to the First Battalion headquarters, promoted to captain, and appointed as a battalion adjutant.

Political Training and the 1962 Coup

The Karen National Union is the political face of the Karen people but, in some areas, commanders had dual duties. They had to represent the KNU because when Karen soldiers went forward into enemy territory or no man's land, they needed to converse or negotiate with locals. Sometimes they went behind enemy lines and people wanted to know the politics of the revolution. So, the military commander had to have some political knowledge to answer people's questions.

Major Shwe Hser and I were given political training in the No.4 Brigade headquarters at Hti Tha Blu Khi. The instructors were Colonel Tin Oo and Padoh Mahn Shan Hpleik from the headquarters of a new department known as the Karen National United Party (KNUP).[4] When the training was over, I was appointed as a column political commissar (policom). I asked a lot of questions during training. The more I learned about politics, the more I knew how to explain it to others.

The military commander, for example, only has to fight, but the policoms have to fight, deal with the civil population and the soldiers, and boost morale. When we went behind enemy lines, we would meet the elders and explain about the revolution and our cause. A policom had to be "a jack of all trades but master of none." When we would explain something, we could not exaggerate because if our speech was too grandiose, some soldiers would say that we were just blowing air. We had to be careful and explain according to the situation. A policom could not praise or criticize, otherwise people would make blowing sounds behind your back and make fun of you.

During the time of the KNUP, Karen political training was similar to that of the communists. At first, I thought that all this was just communist ideology and I didn't take much notice. I thought it was communist ideology because they said we must depend on the masses and deal with them very carefully. The communists also say this. Then I thought it over and realized everyone has to depend on the masses. For example, in elections, all parties are dependent on the vote. This politician will say something, and that politician will say something else, but they are all making these statements to obtain the votes of the people while organizing the masses. The enemy was also organizing the masses. At first, I only looked at it from one side: militarily, not politically. I used to think that you could not organize the masses if you didn't fight. But now I think that you must do both. You must use the left and the right hand. You cannot use only one hand.

The communists from the delta area influenced the Karens. The "P" in KNUP stood for the word "Party." Around this time, there was a lot of discussion about communist ideology and the revolution. They told us not to depend on anyone but the masses, and that when all the masses work together, we will win. Mao Zedong depended on the masses, while the Chinese nationalists,

---

4. Padoh is a Karen honorific used for public officials. Mahn is a Karen honorific equivalent to Mr. in English and is primarily used by Pwo Karens, one of the two main Karen subgroups. The Karen National United Party (KNUP) was formally established in 1953 as a political vanguard party for the KNU. Eventually, left-leaning supporters developed the KNUP as a separate party. This led to a split with the mainstream KNU in the early 1960s that was not resolved until the KNUP's collapse in the mid-1970s.

who were at that time gathering in Taiwan, depended on the United States of America. This was an example for us. Some Karens liked this idea but there was a fear that if the Karens became communists, it would be all about communism, and they would follow foreign leaders like Mao Zedong. It would no longer be about the Karens. There were some who split from the KNU over ideology, and it was later agreed in the mid-1970s that the KNUP would be dissolved and the KNU was enough.[5]

In 1952, I had met Bo Mya, who was a company commander in the Fourth Battalion at the time. He had little formal education but was promoted very quickly and would later become the commander in chief of the KNLA and president of the KNU. He and I were friends. Bo Mya always stuck to his word. If he trusted someone, he always trusted them. But if someone lied to him, he would never trust them again—even if they always told the truth from then onwards. When he married, he converted to Seventh Day Adventist. When we began political training with the KNU in 1953, Bo Mya didn't like it. He was the only one who stood up and opposed joining the communists and becoming the KNUP. People from the delta region automatically formed an alliance with the communists, but Bo Mya said the Karens should be separate from the communists.

In 1956, under KNUP influence, the Kawthoolei Armed Forces was renamed the Karen People's Liberation Army (KPLA). The KAF implied armed forces like a regular army but we were still in a revolution. We were not armed forces yet. We wanted people to understand that we were still fighting for freedom. Our No. 2 Column was converted into the Nineteenth Battalion. Major Shwe Hser was promoted to lieutenant colonel and appointed Nineteenth Battalion commander, and I was then promoted to a major and appointed second-in-command of the Nineteenth Battalion. Shwe Hser was then promoted to colonel and transferred to No. 6 Brigade as brigade commander. My battalion commander was Lieutenant Colonel Daniel.

In 1962 General Ne Win conducted a military coup against the parliamentary government led by Prime Minister U Nu and took over the reins of power. He introduced the Burmese Way to Socialism.[6] With it came a rise in Burman nationalism and heightened discrimination against the other ethnic peoples. When the coup occurred and Ne Win took over power, people had to either run

---

5. The KNUP was more active in the Irrawaddy Delta and Pegu Yoma highland range. After losing its bases in these territories, the KNUP remnants rejoined the KNU in 1976 in the eastern hills. The KNUP was never influential in KNU territories along the Thai border, where Christian leaders like Bo Mya were strongly anticommunist.

6. The Burmese Way to Socialism was a blueprint for economic development that aimed to increase self-reliance and reduce foreign influences in Burma. It eventually drove Burma into poverty and was abandoned in 1988 amid student-led demonstrations for democratic change.

or come to us. But the coup didn't make any difference to us. We believed that individual Burman leaders might rotate, but their strategy toward the Karens would remain the same.

I had first seen U Nu when I was a young boy, as his house was about five hundred yards away from my sister Margaret's house in Rangoon. He was selling some books and I used to go and read at his place. After the coup, he got in contact with the Karens, who asked his people to come and stay with us in Kawthoolei, but he remained in Bangkok.

U Nu, as the former prime minister of Burma, was once an enemy of the Karen people, but in the end he had to make friends with us. He was put under house arrest by Ne Win between 1962 and 1966. Then, following a three-year period spent living in Rangoon, he escaped to the Thai border, where he formed a new armed movement, the Parliamentary Democracy Party (PDP), which allied with us and our Chin and Mon allies in a National United Liberation Front (NULF).[7] But we only trusted him as far as he cooperated with us. There was no close friendship between him and the Karen leaders.

I thought U Nu a smart person politically because he was not like Ne Win who spoke very straight. U Nu could speak very sweetly but you never knew if they were straight or crooked words. People liked to hear him speak, but his words didn't enter their hearts.

I never met Ne Win, but my sisters knew him and his wife Katie. My sister Edna had worked as a secretary for the English manager of Grindlays Bank. Colonel Ne Win, as he was then, used to come into the bank to collect his pay. She used to wear her hair in two plaits. When he came, he would pull on her two plaits. She was afraid of him and didn't dare complain. The other employees said he had a bad reputation as a lady-killer and was known for having mistresses. His wife, Khin May Than (Katie Ba Than), was a friend of my sister Violet. They went to school together. Katie was very beautiful. She spoke English very well and could get on with anybody.

Hunter Thahmwe Goes for Peace Talks

In 1963 Hunter Thahmwe, the then-president of the KNU, went to Rangoon for peace talks, and many soldiers followed Hunter because he was the leader of the

---

7. The allies were the Chin Democracy Party and the New Mon State Party (NMSP). The NMSP is still a close KNU ally today.

KNU. I didn't go with him. I didn't trust the Burmese and I didn't think the war was over yet. When they first arrived in Rangoon, the Burmese media reported falsely that Hunter and the others had surrendered. Later, when the peace talks failed, Hunter did surrender and never returned to the revolution.

Lieutenant Colonel Shwe Hser from the 3rd Battalion didn't go with Hunter either. Shwe Hser contacted us and we became two platoons. We went mobile and traveled around organizing the populace in Hlaingbwe area. I had about thirty soldiers and he had about thirty-three soldiers, so about sixty altogether. Some of the soldiers had gone back to their villages with their arms rather than going with Hunter. We went to village after village to get them to come back. The villagers couldn't understand why we were still going around when some of the army had gone with Hunter for peace talks and everyone was at peace. They thought we were such a small group that we couldn't engage the enemy in the same way. I told them not to worry, that the enemy couldn't destroy our greatest weapon—our morale. If your morale is high, no one will listen to the enemy's propaganda and you can fight at any time. When morale is low, soldiers don't want to fight.

When we traveled around, we met people and asked them to join us. We said we would give them arms when we could get some more, but some said they already had arms and would join us.

Bo Mya was a company commander at that time. His battalion commander had followed Hunter to the peace talks, and he asked Bo Mya to go to Moulmein. There, the Burmese showed him tanks and airplanes and asked if they could really fight them given the equipment the Burmese had. The Burmese thought they knew Bo Mya and considered him ignorant. They thought he would see the tanks and airplanes and surrender. But Bo Mya didn't—he left Moulmein and came back to Kawthoolei. After he went back, the Burmese commander said that he had been tricked by Bo Mya, adding that they had thought that the hill Karens were idiots but now knew that they were smarter than the Burmese.

Bo Mya had gone to Moulmein because his battalion commander asked him to go. He would often tell his troops not to separate; that if we go, we all will go, and if we come back, all of us will come back. If we separate, some people will be left behind. If we all go together, everyone will come back together. This is what happened, and they all came back. When Hunter went, his followers didn't follow him anymore. They were like dogs on an island that couldn't swim.

When Bo Mya came back, we asked him why he went. He said he was angry with the Chinese Kuomintang (KMT), who said they would help but would only fight the Burmese if attacked by them.[8] Bo Mya said that all the KMT

---

8. The Kuomintang (KMT), the Chinese nationalists, entered Burma in 1949–50 after the Communist victory in China (Gibson 2011). By 1953, sixteen thousand KMT troops were in northern Shan

wanted was our pigs and food to eat. He said he would join anyone who wanted to fight the Chinese, but the Burmese were not fighting the Chinese, so he came back. He wanted to go up to Papun to organize more troops. He came from Papun, and the people there were very loyal to him. When dealing with the hill tribes, like Bo Mya you can't change your mind or they won't rely on you anymore. They were happy to join us, and Bo Mya then became the division commander.

Colonel Lin Htin was a Karen battalion commander in Thaton who had gone with Hunter to Rangoon. In Rangoon, he fell in love with and married Louisa Benson, a Jewish Karen who had been crowned Miss Burma twice.[9] There were many rumors that Ne Win was also in love with Louisa. Lin Htin's sister Sadie was friendly with my sisters in Rangoon. Sadie explained that Lin Htin decided to return to the revolution in September 1965. Before he left, they had a party at the Inya Lake Hotel. My sister Edna's mother-in-law, who was a socialite, was there too. At the party, Lin Htin told Sadie, they were surrounded by the Burmese. Lin Htin was able to escape, rumor has it, with the help of the CIA. But he was assassinated by the Burmese in the countryside in Thaton on his return to the revolution. The day after the party many of the guests were arrested or lost their jobs.

After Lin Htin's death, Louisa joined the revolution and became the commander of his First Battalion. She was on the west of the Salween River and I was with the Seventh Brigade on the east. I only met her once, at an annual meeting for battalion commanders. She was very famous and popular with everyone. When Louisa walked in all eyes were on her. She was a great beauty. Everyone had heard about her, that she was a beauty queen, and everyone wanted to see her. I viewed her just like the other women and treated her like any other battalion commander.

When the army was reformed, I went up to the Thai border. Then, when I was traveling around, I went down to the plains again to the Hlaingbwe, Hpa-An, and Moulmein areas. Slowly our column became a battalion, about five hundred altogether, in four companies, each with three platoons of about thirty soldiers. I spent a long time, three or four years, traveling around helping to rebuild the army in these areas.

State (Steinberg and Fan 2012). From there, the KMT attempted to launch attacks into Chinese territory with support from Taiwan and the United States. During this time, some KMT units penetrated as far as Karen-inhabited areas in southeast Burma (Smith 1999, 152–54). The majority of KMT soldiers left Burma for Taiwan after involvement by the United Nations and coordinated Sino-Burmese military operations in 1960–61 (Steinberg and Fan 2012). Some KMT soldiers remained behind along the Thailand border and were closely associated with the drug trade in the area (Chin 2016).

9. Louisa Benson eventually went into exile in the United States, remarried, and became an activist. Her daughter, Charmaine Craig, wrote a novel based on Louisa's life, *Miss Burma* (Craig 2017).

During this time, the name of the KNU armed forces was changed again to the Karen National Liberation Army (KNLA), the name still used today. The main strategic KNLA headquarters was at Manerplaw in a remote region of the Moei River valley adjoining Thailand, but the Tactical Operations Command had a mobile headquarters.

Captain Khin Hlaing was promoted to colonel and appointed No. 4 Brigade Commander. He was so happy when he came to see us and so sad when we left for the frontline because he wanted to join too. It was a big promotion, but he didn't know what to do. Before I was his boss, then he became my boss. His promotion was very quick. He was afraid people would blame him if things went wrong. His family was sick, but he could not look after them, so he was under a lot of pressure. Not long after meeting us, he shot himself.

There were always changes in the situation with the officers because people died. We were promoted quickly, and we had to push up quickly. We had to be ready to shuffle according to the situation.

Nineteenth Battalion Commander

In 1968, I was promoted to lieutenant colonel and was appointed Nineteenth Battalion commander. My job was commanding infantry on the frontline. At that time, we did joint operations for three to four months at a time.

During the Burmese Way to Socialism, Ne Win weakened the Karen masses through forced relocation under a ruthless military strategy known as the Four Cuts.[10] By relocating the people, they tried to take away the water (the Karen people) from the fish (the KNLA) who depended on it for food and survival. The Burmese sold all the rice to foreigners so the masses could not eat, and relocated the Karen people to places near the Burmese towns.

But the Karens got rice from Thailand, and our soldiers went to the new villages. The hill people were able to dig underground and grow root vegetables as big as pumpkins. They would wash and slice them, put them in baskets, and keep them in the water. They would then put the vegetables in a pot to steam and cook and were able to eat this in place of rice. It was filling but gave no strength. So the Karen villagers ate rice once every three days and then ate the root vegetables the other days.

---

10. After being rolled out across different ethnic nationality regions of the country in subsequent decades, this policy has become internationally notorious. The practice has been well documented by Amnesty International and multiple nongovernmental and United Nations human rights agencies, leading to calls for army leaders to be brought before the International Criminal Court (Amnesty International 2019: 28; United Nations Human Rights Council 2018: 15–16).

When we went around to the villages, everyone, including all the officers, carried rice bags on our backs. We bought the rice from merchants in Thailand using money collected from the customs gates. We asked for a big pot from the village and boiled up water and put rice in. When it was cooked, we mixed coconut in and all the children came around to eat. But our soldiers had to eat the root vegetables. After three days we needed to eat rice or we would have no strength to fight. We only ate rice in the jungle, though, because we couldn't eat rice in front of the children.

When there was a military operation, the Karen ex-soldiers or some other villagers would ask us whether we had surplus arms and they would serve for one operation. After the operation they would give back the arms and go back home. In the 1980s, mercenaries and soldiers of fortune would occasionally volunteer just for one operation. Japanese, French, and Australian fighters came to help. We liked the Japanese who came to fight because they brought new weapons and left them for us when they went back to Japan. The other foreign volunteers used our weapons and gave them back to us when they left. They came on their own expense and came to fight just for fun and to experience combat.

Time passed quickly on the front. My role as an operations commander under general headquarters was difficult. I liked this job because it was about knowing your men, your enemy, and the Karen masses, and what was feasible and what was not. Sometimes I knew some plans would lead to the death of some of my men. In fighting, you knew soldiers would get killed but you never knew how many. You had to estimate the least number that could be killed. Sometimes there were few casualties and other times there were more than I expected. It is rare to be hit during guerrilla warfare because you are not fighting from one position and the enemy can't pinpoint you. Instead you wait in ambush to surprise the enemy and so you have the upper hand. Our motto was "shoot the enemy first and don't miss."

6

FAMILY

I met Tharamu Naw Sheera Ba Tin while I was working in the Hlaingbwe area in the late 1950s.[1] Our unit was a mobile column moving from township to township in Hpa-An district. I met Sheera in Paing Kyon village, also known as Ta Kreh, where she was a teacher. She was the daughter of Saw Ba Tin and Naw Mae Mae of Et Et village, Tavoy district. I admired her and fell in love.

After a few years I decided to marry her. At first, I kept my decision to myself and didn't even tell Sheera. I had thought that only when there was peace in the country, when we achieved Kawthoolei, would I settle down; otherwise I would stay a bachelor.

The higher authorities were responsible for marriage arrangements. There was a rule: if anyone in the revolution intended to get married, they must report to a higher authority at least one year before the wedding date. The KNLA always organized to have one or two weddings at the same time because it was easier.

I made my request and Brigadier Elmo Peel replied that the wedding would be on January 20, 1961, at Kamahta Village. I wrote a letter to Sheera through Padoh Ba Chit who was chairman of Paing Kyon township. Brigadier Elmo's wife was so excited to hear I was getting married. She had studied with my elder sisters Anne and Violet in Moulmein; she was friendly with them and treated me like a brother. She told me to go and see Sheera and tell her about

---

1. Tharamu (also spelt Thramu) means teacher in Sgaw Karen language.

the wedding in person, in case when the school closed she had gone home to her parents in Et Et village. I told her it was still early.

On the January 19, 1961, I went down to Hlaingbwe area to fetch a ring and clothes for our wedding. It was a very long journey to go and come back on foot the same day to Kamahta village. I had to cross enemy territory to get there and it was quite treacherous.

The night before the wedding there was a concert. I heard Padoh Saw Taw (the master of ceremony) announce after the concert, don't go home yet because tomorrow there will be a big wedding ceremony for three couples. Mrs. Elmo Peel asked me whether Sheera had arrived. I told her I hadn't seen her yet. She was so anxious and reminded me that she had told me to go personally and meet her. "You only wrote a letter. What if she didn't get the letter and doesn't come? The wedding is tomorrow. What will you do about it?" she asked. I told her calmly, "We can announce if there is anyone who would like to marry me, they can do so. Everything is ready." She got so annoyed, she told me "Don't be an idiot! Who is going to be that silly!"

On January 20, the day of the wedding, I asked Padoh Ba Chit about Sheera. He told me to wait a moment then opened his briefcase, and I saw that my letter for Sheera was still there, not yet delivered! He had forgotten all about it. Sheera knew nothing about the wedding. Only two couples were married that day.

The authorities concerned fixed a new date, January 31, 1961, but I insisted it be February 1 because January 31 is Karen Revolution Day, and I had to give a speech at the ceremony. We couldn't get married on that day.

On January 31, many people came for a ceremonial parade, where the soldiers marched past and saluted the Karen national flag and the people bowed in respect. There were many speeches about the Karen Revolution. Mine was on behalf of the army. The administration representative and some of the local leaders also gave speeches.

On the February 1, 1961, Sheera and I at last got married at Pway Htaw Roe village. After we were married, we stayed together for a few days before I had to return to the frontline. I didn't come home for six months.

I didn't write any letters to Sheera because this would put the person carrying the letter at risk. The best thing I could do was to keep my mouth shut and let her contact me if she needed to. I would come back for a week or so at the time then I would go away for a few months or sometimes years. I could only come back when the situation was right. If there is no important operation, then I could come back; but it depended on whether our mission was long or short.

It took a while for Sheera to get pregnant. The wife of Tun Kyaing, another officer, was also taking a long time to get pregnant. We would joke that we should put them both in a hut with a tiger outside until they got pregnant. Sheera finally became pregnant and had our first child, a son called Dey Law, while I was away. I was so happy when I heard she had had the baby. I grew up in a big family and I always wanted a big family of my own.

I had a few days off and went home to visit Sheera and my new son. Dey Law was only one week old. I saw my son for a few days before I went back to a meeting in Papun. Dey Law slept between the two of us. One day I was sleeping with the baby, while Sheera was doing something and the baby cried. Sheera came and took him away. When I woke up, I didn't see Dey Law. I looked through the bamboo floor to see if he had fallen through. She asked what I was looking for, and I replied I was looking for the baby!

I didn't like small babies—they look funny and behave funny. I would avoid going to houses with small babies. Whenever Sheera asked me to carry a baby I wouldn't look at their faces.

Sheera didn't have any family or friends around to support her so it was difficult on her own with a new baby. When my son was only a few months old, he got malaria and died. I didn't expect him to die. I thought that when I went back again, I'd see him. I was excited to see my first son again but when I arrived home, I discovered he had died. I only got to spend a few days with him.

My wife told me that she didn't know what to do. She told me not to feel bad as she didn't blame me and she couldn't blame herself. It was her first child and she didn't know what to do when the baby got malaria since there was no hospital and no family or friends around to help her, only strangers.

All the villagers, all the soldiers—no one was free from malaria. We were only free from malaria when we arrived in Australia. Everybody had malaria throughout their lives. Some people died from malaria. Some people, especially the hill tribes, used some sort of herbal medicine from a tree bark. It was very bitter, but they would boil it and drink the water, which was what my wife did. When you are a recruit with malaria, you shiver, you get boiling hot, you sweat, and after sweating you get better. When you become a regular soldier you have built up resistance and suffer less from the disease. If you live to be an old soldier, you are used to it and you don't feel anything. When small children have malaria, after sweating they recover and go straight to the kitchen and start eating. Malaria and hepatitis were the main diseases we faced during the revolution.

My second son, Ler Paw (John), was born in 1965, also while I was away. When I arrived home, one of the soldiers carried him on his shoulders and asked me if I knew the child. By looking at him I knew he was my son. But by the time I met him he was already talking. While I was away, sometimes I would think of my wife and children but most of the time my mind was occupied with work. My third son, Ler Gay (James), was born in 1968, and my first daughter, Mina, was born in 1971.

FIGURE 5.   Mina in Maesot, 1982

After we were married, both Sheera and I felt that we were married but lived like bachelors. The Burmese say, "When you get married you can't go about freely." The Burmese word for marriage literally means "house jail." But Sheera and I were still going about freely; we were married so we could not behave as bachelors, but I was not at home so we weren't living as a married couple either.

When I came home and saw Sheera I was happy to be home with my family, but at the same time I felt sad that I had been away for so long and we wasted so much time apart. Each time I left, we didn't know when I would come back. Over time, coming, going, and being apart became very normal. As an officer, I had to set an example for other soldiers. When they looked at me, they dared not ask for leave. Some officers went back to their families regularly. So, when their soldiers asked for leave and were refused, they would say, "What about you?"

When we were on the move we would pass through some villages where our soldiers had family. We would stay outside the village without their families knowing and would leave before dawn. My soldiers would ask to visit their families in the village, but I told them they couldn't go because when the group was on the move we didn't want people to know we were there. If one person went into the village, news would spread of our location, which could bring trouble for the village and for us. I told them that when we go home, we must go home openly and leave openly. Sometimes we stopped for the night near where Sheera was living, but I didn't go to see her. She would feel hurt and ask why I didn't come and say hello. I told her that I couldn't go home because my soldiers couldn't go home; I didn't want to have double standards.

Later, when I worked in the KNLA's headquarters in Manerplaw, Sheera lived in a nearby village where other officer's families lived. Every Friday evening, the officers would go home to their families. Only the duty officers would stay behind. I often stayed behind because I was used to being separated from my family. I would stay so others could go home. Some soldiers like to gossip about those officers who go home every week.

When I did go home, life would be normal. The revolution would support families with some supplies, but we had to do our own farming. Sheera raised pigs, goats, chickens, and ducks that she could use for food or to sell. We had to cultivate dry farming, using methods like "slash and burn." Slash and burn farming is very tough because you are busy no matter the weather. With rice, the fields are empty after the harvest, so you can rest. But with slash and burn it is around the clock. There was no rest when we came home, for I had to help. We used leaves and bamboo for building and repairing thatched roofs. While I was away, Sheera had to struggle with all this on her own.

FIGURE 6. Senior officers in Manerplaw, KNU GHQ 1980 (Ralph standing in the middle of the second row; Major Aaron, far left with glasses; General Tamlar Baw below Ralph; and Colonel Gladstone on his right)

Cutting bamboo seems easy but it is not. Sometimes just to repair the house I spent the whole day collecting bamboo and came back with only one or two bamboo stalks. Sheera would ask where the rest were. I told her I couldn't bring the rest, because I used to choose the straight bamboo, not the tender ones. The straight bamboo is surrounded by other bamboo, so I would have to clear the rest to get to it. Then it would get tangled with the creepers, so you couldn't pull it out. Villagers, when they went to cut bamboo, could collect twenty or thirty stalks in one hour. They would find the best place, cut them all, tie them together, and push them so they would all fall. Then they'd choose what they wanted from the pile. For me, I couldn't get at them after cutting them and I couldn't carry them all. There is a knack to collecting bamboo that they had but I didn't.

Of my five children, I was only at home for the birth of my last child, Paw Nay Thah (Judith), in 1973 in Kler Thay Lu in Thailand. We all had to make sacrifices. At first, before meeting Sheera, I thought I would not get married to anyone because my children would need to be independent of their father in case we were defeated. I thought I would wait until the war was over before starting a family. After I met Sheera and I had children, I didn't want them to go through hardship, but everyone has to go through hardship. Children learn from hardship, which is good preparation for life.

The KNU paid for the education of the soldiers' children, who could either go to school close to their parents' house or study elsewhere, such as a boarding school run by the KNU. My cousin Tabu's son Ler Pwe Po came to study in Manerplaw and his mother asked me to keep him as my son because it was a long and dangerous journey between their home and Manerplaw. I agreed, and he stayed with me.

I didn't care whether my sons joined the army or not. It was their choice. My eldest son John became a Forest Armed Guard. When there was fighting they became soldiers, otherwise they protected the forest. During the revolution, when the Burmese attacked, Saw Ler Gay, my youngest son, and Sheera would help with supplies like water and rice. After the battle was over, they would go back to their normal lives.

With my daughters, they could also choose their own careers. My daughter Mina wanted to become a pastor and she did. When she was studying, she was one of twenty selected to come to Australia. She stayed with my brother Howard and his family in Perth, where he had emigrated to in 1968. Mina was interested in religion, and when she finished her studies, she went to Riverview Bible College in Perth.

I was happy I married Sheera because she understood all our difficulties. She didn't grumble. She knew that even if she grumbled, she still had to face it, so why grumble if you cannot avoid it?

REVOLUTION HEADQUARTERS

In 1970 I was posted to general headquarters in Manerplaw as general staff offi-cer number two (G2). I worked in the Intelligence Branch. I was in charge of intelligence from General Headquarters (GHQ) down to the battalion level. My commander was the general staff officer number one (G1), Colonel Marvel, who found Manerplaw too cold so went to Bangkok to work in foreign affairs. In 1974, I was promoted to G1 as a full colonel to take his place. I didn't care about the weather. I was only forty-four years old. As G1 I was the chief military strategist for the KNLA and in charge of operations, training, intelligence, and signals, which were grouped in the General Branch (G Branch) for which I was responsible. I was reporting directly to the general officer in command, Chief of Staff General Bo Mya, who also became president of the KNU in 1976. General Tamlar Baw was his vice chief of staff. As G1, I was also a member of the general officer in command's War Council. The Quartermaster Branch (Q Branch) and Administration Branch (A Branch) also reported to the chief of staff and vice chief of staff. The adjunct general, the quartermaster general, and I were later all promoted to the rank of brigadier general. I had to do more political training when I was a brigadier. Later, not long before Manerplaw fell, I also became a KNU committee member.

As a G1 I was looking for intelligence about the Burmese, the communists, and everyone else. Members of the Thai army and some retired American officers from the Korean or Vietnam War taught us about intelligence and how to collect it. We had spies who kept an eye on the enemy. We exchanged intelligence with the Thai army. We would meet them at the border, drink with them the whole

FIGURE 7. 1981 KNU Calendar

day, and share information. Thailand bordered the Burmese and the Karen, so they dealt with everyone. Their policy was not to only be friends with one side.

It was my job to know what was going on. By gathering all the available information, we could be better prepared to expect what might happen. My staff dealt with everybody to get information. Our men collected information and then with the information we interrogated people. We did not torture them, because torture makes people speak blindly, and the information is not useful.

There were many sorts of people to source information from. With the decline of the Burmese economy, there was a lot of cross-border trade between Burma and Thailand, and our men would talk with these traders. Sometimes we didn't even have to ask; they would just give us information because they sympathized with the revolution, which they couldn't join but could help. Not all of the traders were Karen so they had to be careful as they feared reprisals against their families.

We kept all the information we got, which we processed, crosschecked, evaluated, and disseminated to the relevant people. I learned this procedure from an American ex-serviceman. Once the informant gave us the information, we were responsible for determining its accuracy and value. We listened to all informants and accepted everyone and everything.

The Burmese army frequently tried to trick us with misinformation. For example, two Burmese army deserters might tell us something, but if their stories were

FIGURE 8. Colonel Ralph (second from right, back row) and office team (posing) in Manerplaw

different, we would be suspicious. If the traitor was one of our own agents, we noticed if they felt freer to go about their business and thus were unlikely to be trustworthy.

We also got intelligence from captured soldiers. Many of the enemy we captured were so frightened of us they immediately told us everything we wanted to know. When the Burmese captured Karen soldiers, they too were frightened and often told the enemy everything.

I didn't really enjoy working in intelligence, but sometimes it was interesting. In this work, it is important that everyone be well trained and work together. If a new person does things differently, he needs to explain to the others and share his knowledge. We needed to be like a football team: the better you coordinate with each other the faster you can achieve your goals.

Signals intelligence is about intercepting enemy messages, decoding and deciphering them, and maintaining secrecy. We had to keep changing our codes. If we were planning an operation, we worked out where to attack, how many soldiers were needed, and what to do next. We planned the route, time frame, and what supplies were needed. We gave the soldiers their orders, prepared for the operation, and, only then when they were leaving, gave them the code: one code for one battle. When the revolution began we had a radio with a small antenna, but bit by bit communications got smaller as technology improved. The ciphers came from our office where a special group created the codes.

As G1, I was in charge of all army training. At first the majority of the Karens were British trained; some even went to Sandhurst.[1] Slowly some Burma army soldiers came over to us and taught us. Some of the staff I trained are still working today; others left during the ceasefire that was agreed to in 2012.

The most important part of training concerned shooting, attacking, and withdrawing. Tactics depended on the officers and their ability. Those who just obeyed and didn't think didn't rise quickly, but they were still good soldiers. A soldier's duty is to obey. Those who were smart and learned fast rose quickly. They put their training into practice when out on patrol, relying on their knowledge, experience, and abilities.

Our soldiers learned how to survive in jungle warfare. Sometimes Thai Special Forces taught our people skills. Once, after training our men on survival skills for about ten days, they said that they wanted to return to Thailand. When we asked why, they told us that the Karen soldiers knew more than they did. The Karens had better knowledge of what sort of things you can eat in the jungle. In books there may be a dozen ways to survive, but the Karens know hundreds. American soldiers also tried to teach us how to survive behind enemy lines, and they said the same as the Thai soldiers. But they kept on teaching us because they were learning from our soldiers.

On the operations side of my role, we planned strategies, then let commanders in the field plan their own tactics. I used the strategies I had learned from my time in the battlefield. For this operational planning we would assess the situation and work out the best line of attack, the soldiers and supplies that would be needed, and the number of days we expected the operation to take. We would ask the adjunct general (head of A Branch) and the quartermaster general (head of Q Branch) about the soldiers and supplies. After we had sent off the operational plan to the general officer in command, Chief of Staff Bo Mya, the vice chief of staff Tamlar Baw, and I would then discuss the plan and agree to it or make changes. We would then convene the War Council with the adjunct general and quartermaster general, who, after everyone had agreed to the plan, would arrange for troops and supplies. Then the operation was ready to begin.

Of my areas of responsibilities as G1, I preferred operations because we were more involved in what was happening on the battlefield. I would just listen and see how I could support the fighters. A commander would be responsible for a particular operation. The problem with the office was too much of the same administrative work, whereas the front line was exciting with lots of different things going on. I would often go to the front line for one or two days; it was more enjoyable being out in the field.

---

1. The Royal Military Academy Sandhurst is the British Army's premier officer training center.

The revolution's headquarters, Manerplaw, means "Victory Field." It was protected by the Salween River to the west and the Moei River to the east and surrounded by rocky hills, particularly the rugged Dawna mountain ranges to the west and south. Our army built the town out of the jungle. Manerplaw was a military, not a civilian, town, although there were some businesses run by soldiers' families.

The buildings in Manerplaw were made of timber and were single-story. Only the KNU president's house was two stories, brick below and timber above. All the roads were gravel or dirt. There was one long street along the Moei River, on which the KNU, the training department, and the signals and intelligence departments were situated.

The village of Htoo Wah Lu, where Sheera and many of the officers' families lived, was down the road on the Thai side of the border. To the north of the GHQ was a guesthouse for foreigners, and next to the guesthouse was the administration. The GHQ was essentially an assortment of huts with timber frames and flooring. The buildings were perched on stilts above the ground, so people—and animals—could go under them. Every department had its own building, and military and political functions were separate. There was a church for all the Christian denominations, and the Buddhists had a temple on the other side of the river.

FIGURE 9. A popular transport mode on border (Ralph, dismounted, standing left of truck)

FIGURE 10. Ralph at home in Htoo Wah Lu, 1986

Some of the generals in the revolution were serious about church, while others like me weren't. We knew that there was a God and that if we needed anything we had to pray. Because we didn't have Bible studies, we only knew what the pastor preached.

While we were in Manerplaw we lived and ate at the Officers' Quarters. The office was in front, then the bedrooms, and behind was the kitchen. The Officers' Quarters had a wood floor with plywood walls. Food was rice, fish paste, chili, and vegetables, but usually no meat. If you wanted meat you had to wait until you went home. Farming was difficult in that area because it was in the war zone, so meat had to be raised elsewhere or bought from Thailand, which was expensive.

There was a football ground in Manerplaw. Later they built another larger football ground and the first one became a place for evening roll call. I used to play and watch football.

To relax, we used to take our rifles and go out into the jungle to shoot animals or birds to cook and eat. I used to go with one or two soldiers but sometimes I would hunt alone. If I shot something, I would tell someone where it was and they would go and fetch it for me.

Bo Mya was a good hunter who loved shooting—and eating—birds. He would go hunting with a few soldiers who would make a small fire for him to cook what he shot. He was quite stocky, so these hunting expeditions were about weight loss. Climbing the mountains with a 0.22 rifle, he would sweat and maybe lose some weight. But it was also his way to relax. One morning he shot fifteen or twenty small birds. He was going to bring them to the GHQ, but instead he ate them all on the way back.

I used to drink a lot during the revolution. We were always on the move, and when we got to some villages, they would always be celebrating a wedding or calling the spirits and would coax us to take a little drink. Then I started drinking a lot. Whenever friends had alcohol, they would call the others, and we would all drink together.

When I was drinking, I drank and drank. I didn't think of the future and had an "enjoy yourself while you're alive" sort of attitude. We didn't know who was going to die or when. At any moment any of us could die, so I may as well have a good time while I'm still alive.

We drank all the time. One time, my brother Howard from Australia was visiting, and we were driving somewhere. We stopped and got some drinks and did the same at the next town. The car was overheating, so I sent one of the young soldiers to find water, and he was taking so long to come back, we decided to go. Howard asked, "What about that boy?" I said that he'd find his way back. Howard then asked if he'd been here before. We said no, so Howard pleaded for us to wait till he came back. The soldiers must have wondered who this guy was, telling the colonel to wait! Howard felt terrible about leaving this boy while we kept drinking.

Many of the officers used to drink; we were all fish from the same ocean. Some could hold their liquor while others couldn't. I could hold my liquor and still function. My brother once asked Bo Mya what he thought of my drinking. Bo Mya said, "Oh, he does his job better when he drinks; he gets more information from people."

By nature, the Karens are very tongue-tied, quiet, and they don't socialize. They have a saying: "Karens learn to hold water in their mouths." The only way to get them to talk is to get them to drink and then the information will flow.

It was very hard to deal with hill Karens because they don't have much to say. It's difficult to get them to engage, so we would offer them a bottle of rice wine. First, they would share one cup, all taking a sip. After about two or three cups, they would start talking, and we would become friends, and they would tell us things.

So, to deal with people you had to deal with rice wine. I got used to it. In the hills they would not sell wine, they would just give it to us. In one village, if one house didn't have it, we would go next door, and so on.

Our lives were quite social. We used to sit around telling jokes with the soldiers and the officers. We all used to sit around on chairs on the front verandah of the Officer's Quarters and tell jokes and laugh. People say that laughter is good for your health. If you are sad and lonely you are damaging your health so you must laugh at least once a day. We didn't laugh every day but most days.

We would get visitors off and on in Manerplaw. They would come and stay for two or three days; we had lots of people staying around the clock in the Officer's Quarters. If my boss Tamlar Baw didn't go home on the weekend, we would sit around and crack jokes together.

Major Aaron was another good friend with whom I also cracked jokes. He was an old British soldier from the Burma navy. When World War II broke out, the British needed men from Burma to go behind enemy lines. So, he parachuted back into Japanese-occupied Burma and collected intelligence to send back to the British. He stayed near Karen villages in the hills and people had to take him food. He was not allowed to come into the village because if information leaked out about him and his work, there would be reprisals.

When the revolution started, Aaron volunteered and he rose to battalion commander and lieutenant colonel. He then followed Hunter Thahmwe for peace talks. When he returned, Bo Mya demoted him back to soldier and told Aaron that when he followed Hunter, his lieutenant colonel rank was given to (former prime minister) U Nu, so Aaron had to start again from the bottom ranks. Aaron told Bo Mya that he didn't mind starting over again. He would joke that he was not an "ordinary" soldier but an "honorary" soldier. He rose to a major but he stayed mainly in the records office.

Battles for the Customs Gates

Taxes at the customs gates on the Thai border were an important source of income for the KNU and KNLA. Before the 1990s, the enemy would typically attack for about a week and then retreat. The usual target was one of the main customs gates at Wangkha. The whole of Burma used that gate, especially to transport minerals from Kachin State to be sold on the Thai side. The income collected every day at Wangkha was massive—several hundred thousand Thai baht (tens of thousands of US dollars) each day. At Wangkha and Palu, merchants traded minerals on a big scale. Other gates were small, with only cattle, buffaloes, sheep, and pigs going through, so the Burmese didn't take much notice of them.

In Karen State they used Thai baht and Burmese kyat but in Thailand they didn't like Burmese kyat because there were too many notes. The Thai didn't accept them and you could not change them. So, they would use Thai baht, which they could take to other gates and exchange.

At that time, if you exchanged foreign currency legally in Burma, one US dollar equaled 6 Kyats. But on the black market, one US dollar equaled hundreds of Kyats. This was a vast difference, so everyone exchanged on the black market rather than legally.

In September 1980, I was at the General Headquarters in Manerplaw when the enemy Forty-Fourth Light Infantry Division was deployed to seize the customs gate at Mae Ta Waw, opposite Tha Song Yang village on the Thai side of the Moei River. Our army signals intelligence intercepted a message that the enemy had already advanced to Klau Ka Ti (also known as Shan Ywa Thit).

Captain Tennor was a company commander and a customs officer with dual duty at the gate. Saw Charles was his second in command. They had a company of soldiers attached for the defense of the gate and security measures.

As soon as Captain Tennor got word that the Burmese were going to attack, he reported to the GHQ for more reinforcements and ammunition supplies. Meanwhile, Saw Charles hid his men along the side of the road, so they could ambush the enemy when they came past. He took with him one quarter of the soldiers.

Bo Mya told Tamlar Baw to send one of the senior officers to inspect the gate before the enemy attacked to see if everything was ready. We had a little over a hundred men, already reduced by one quarter, set to ambush. General Tamlar Baw thought the gate might fall because the Burmese were going to attack with three battalions—about 1,500 men.

General Tamlar Baw called me and asked me to go and see what was happening. He believed they would ask for reinforcements but he knew we had none. He told me that if we needed to withdraw, I, being a hunter and knowing all the creeks and valleys to follow, could manage the retreat. I didn't argue. I set off from Manerplaw, escorted by long tail boats. It was raining and it got dark on the way. I sneaked into Thailand and arranged some elephants, and we continued our night march.

The weather was bad; it rained the whole way there. When we arrived at Mae Ta Waw at dawn, the rain had stopped. I sent for Captain Tennor and handed over the ammunition. We had a brief talk about the situation. While we were talking, the enemy started firing some mortar smoke bombs, for range finding. Then the high explosive bombs followed. Since the rain had stopped, the geographical features were in clear view. It was a good opportunity for both sides.

Captain Tennor requested that I stay with him during the battle and advise him. I told him to ask the GHQ because I only had orders to deliver ammunition. The GHQ agreed that I should join him in battle.

They had already been shelling our position for two days before we arrived. Fortunately, Major Yaw Mu and his column had harassed the Burmese behind enemy lines, on their way between Hti Thay Khi and Mae Ta Waw. Saw Charles contacted Major Yaw Mu and combined with his column. Unfortunately, though, they could not harass the enemy in an organized way.

On the third day, the Burmese infantry engaged our troops. On the frontal attack were the Burmese Forty-Fourth Light Infantry Division commandos. On our right flank at Hti Lay Hta, was the light infantry battalion and our left flank at Mae Pawhha was the Thirty-Fifth Elite Battalion from Taungoo.

As soon as the enemy approached the killing ground, the rain started to pour down. The opportunity was ours. Our troops were in the overhead bunkers, while the enemy was in the midst of the obstacles, booby traps, and land mines. The terrain was full of steep, rocky cliffs with a couple of passes and just a few tiny footpaths on it.

The enemy commandos charged several times at our frontal defense, but each time we beat them back. The enemy couldn't advance any further: neither on our left nor on our right flanks. They were pinned down.

On the day before the battle started, I saw many Karen officers and other ranks from various units at the command post come as spectators to watch the battle. On the second day they started leaving because of the enemy, weather, and terrain. The enemy had an overwhelming numerical superiority over the KNLA and the weather was rainy all along, but the terrain was good for our troops. The problem was that the enemy was in front and the Moei River at our rear, so withdrawal was out of the question. The spectators became critical of the situation, so they gave up hope and left.

Brigadier Padoh Baw Yu Paw came to visit us. I asked him to stay with us till the battle was over; he agreed and remained.

We could only evacuate our wounded at night, which was the only time our food and supplies could also be brought in. When our rice and curry got to us at midnight, we had to eat it at once, while it was warm, whether we were hungry or not. We kept the leftovers for another meal for midday, even though sometimes it got stale, packaged in little plastic bags secured with rubber bands. But we otherwise had to wait till midnight for the next meal. On the fifth day, Captain Tennor felt he was in over his head and asked Padoh Baw Yu Paw and me to grant him a few days leave, which we did.

The enemy formed a crescent with the Moei River at the rear. Our signals intelligence intercepted an enemy radio order: "Operation order from Forty-Fourth Division; the battalion from the right flank is to attack the Karen command post within the perimeter of the gate and fight fiercely and seize it. The frontal commando is to strike hard and press fiercely to drive out Karen troops to our left flank. Thirty-Fifth Elite Battalion is to fix bayonets and stay in wait. When Karen troops disperse, conduct fierce hand-to-hand combat."

On hearing this information, some officers and other ranks immediately deserted their posts, so with only about a platoon (thirty people) left, Padoh Baw Yu Paw and I visited all our positions and encouraged the remaining troops to fight to the last.

The weather was very bad. Because of heavy rain and rough terrain, they had to move along the streams. It was a hard time for the enemy. We had bunkers, but they stayed in the rain. They had to come all the way from the Hlaingbwe River. It was normally a stream, but the rain turned it into a big river. The water was over their heads. Their food and ammunition supplies could not get to them and they were getting low on supplies. They asked the porters to chop some wild banana plants for them to eat.[2] After two or three days there were no banana plants left, so they had to find some other food.

The Burmese command sent the withdrawal order through a special runner system, but they could not get in touch with each other. The frontal commandos and the Thirty-Fifth Elite Battalion finally received the withdraw order. After about a week the enemy started to withdraw, one battalion at a time.

Owing to the extreme weather, the Tactical Operations command lost radio contact with their right flank, the Lay Daw combat troops, who never received withdrawal orders. The last orders they received were to attack, so they attacked. Our right flank also attacked them while our left flank lay still and did not fire. Our right flank was pressing hard with hand-to-hand fighting.

That evening the enemy managed to enter the gate. There were only twelve or thirteen of us left. All the rest had disappeared. I put those that remained in positions around the gate. I ordered six men to go from the left flank and shoot from the side.

Our six men began firing. The enemy company commander tried to encourage his soldiers and was shot and killed. The enemy got to the top of the hill and began firing at our six men where their backs were exposed. Two were killed and two were wounded, the remaining two carried the others. The four of us who resisted from the front had no casualties.

As soon as our men opened fire from the flank the enemy gave a tremendous covering fire, but quickly retreated. On their way back they made contact with the special runners and received the withdrawal order. The whole battalion was then on full retreat to Thaton.

I thought everything was achieved not by us but by God. Everything was on our side, including the weather. Although our reinforcements could not take on the enemy from any side, the flooded river helped us. It was raining day and night and the enemy supplies could not cross the river. So, with few supplies and their ammunition running down, the enemy had to withdraw.

Two days after the battle I went back to Manerplaw. Padoh Baw Yu Paw and I were going to be awarded the gallantry medal. I rejected it and I told Padoh Baw

2. For military operations in the hills, the Burmese army routinely conscripted civilian porters, often in large numbers, to carry supplies and ammunition onto the front line. It was an internationally condemned practice in which many porters died during the 1980s and 1990s especially.

Yu Paw, "Let the four people that stayed there and the six people who stayed with me have medals. The two of us won't take the medals. Just let the six boys have them to encourage them."

I told him not to take it because it would cheapen it, as it did at Wangkha. During the first battle at Wangkha, there were some Karen people on the Thai side of the border, just watching the battle from a safe position. When I went there, I stayed across the river at the front line. When the battle was over, everyone was awarded medals, including those people who were just spectators. The medal was cheapened, so I didn't want one. When they gave me a medal I said that I wouldn't take it because I just went to visit and I wasn't authorized to fight.

In my career, I was offered five medals, but only took three. One is the Karen Revolutionary Star because I was in the revolution from the beginning all the way through. One is for infantry, which is nickel-plated; the Revolutionary Star is silver; and the one for long service is gold.

In the second battle for Mae Ta Waw, in 1984, the enemy overran it. Later, our troops counterattacked and regained it and held it for some time. At the third battle, the enemy attacked, took it, and still occupies it today.

My Family Comes to Find Me

Margaret's daughter, my niece Maureen, was the first to find me in the jungle in 1980. When I left home, she was in a cradle. When she came to find us, she kept inquiring with relatives about me until step by step she found one in Mae Sot who sent for me, telling me that one of my nieces had come to see me. We went with the truck: four or five of us with some of our soldiers. When I went to the safe house, Maureen was looking at us, wondering which one was her uncle, while I was wondering which one was my niece. We went aside together and talked for a long time. We were both so happy to see each other.

Maureen told me that my father had passed away in 1960. He wasn't that old, but had died of heart failure. He went to stay with my mother's youngest sister, Mae Mae, in Kalaw, as he said that he always wanted to die in Kalaw, up in the hills with the fresh air.

Later on, Maureen brought her mother, Margaret, my eldest sister, to see me in Manerplaw. I was so happy; I hadn't expected to see my siblings again, but I reunited with them one by one. They told each other how to find me and some came to Mae Sot to meet me, including Wilbur, my elder brother who had been in the Burmese army.

In 1985 I got hepatitis and was sent to Bangkok for treatment. A soldier who spoke Thai accompanied me to act as my batman, or assistant, as well as interpreter. Sheera didn't come with me because it was arranged by the army. The doctor knew me from when he was posted in Mae Sot. First, he asked me to go and stay with his mother near the airport. It was quite noisy and every two minutes a plane would come or go and shake everything around me. So he told me to move to Chiang Mai because it would be far away from the airport.

In Chiang Mai I stayed in the house of a Thai friend from Mae Sot. The doctor told me not to think of my work or anything that troubled my mind. He also told me to walk up to the monastery on the hill, to pass my time and to relax. In the morning I would walk up there before coming back to the house to eat. My friend's wife used to boil a dozen quail eggs every day. I'd never eaten them before and really liked them. She also used to barbeque the quail, which was very tasty. She used to sell the quails and quail eggs in the market, but the more I ate, the fewer she had to sell, so we were both very happy. In the evening I would go back up to the monastery on the hill to watch the lights of Chiang Mai. I found the walks really did clear my mind and it was very relaxing. This was the first time since the revolution began that I lived somewhere where there was peace.

After two months I asked the doctor if I could go and visit Mae Sot. He didn't like the idea, saying that if I went there, I would talk about my work. I promised I wouldn't ask about my work, but he knew that my friends would tell me. In the end, I went back to Kawthoolei anyway.

In 1986 my brother Howard followed my other relatives and came to visit me. He came while I was in Palu, at church. I came out, chewing betel nut and spitting it out. When they told Howard I was his brother, he didn't believe them. We returned to Manerplaw and Htoo Wah Lu, where he stayed for a few weeks.

The last time I had seen Howard, we were in Insein, at the beginning of the revolution. My father had sent him, Edna, Maureen, and Fanny to India with Florence and her family, because he was afraid there would be reprisals against Karens. Many Anglo-Karens were moving overseas and it was easiest to go to India. My siblings didn't like India and returned to Burma a few years later. Howard's education had largely been in English and it had been interrupted by all the fighting. His Burmese was not sufficient to pass the university entrance exam and he wanted to find a way to go to England, so in 1955, when he was eighteen, he followed my brothers Jack and Wilbur into the Burmese armed forces. They sent him to the UK to do his apprenticeship as an aeroelectrician at the Royal Air Force in Buckinghamshire. Afterwards he did an apprenticeship and gained some experience before returning to Burma in 1959. He married a Karen named Esther and they had four children. He worked in aircraft maintenance for the Burmese air force for almost ten years, but faced racism and could not progress. In 1968 his family jumped at the chance to emigrate to Australia. They arrived in Perth in April 1969, where they have lived ever since. They later had a fifth child.

I hadn't seen him for almost forty years. To see him again was like a dream come true, because neither of us thought we would meet each other again. When he came to Manerplaw, Howard tried to hide the fact that he had served in the Burmese air force, but someone recognized him. Despite this, people were nice to him and he stayed for a month. He joined me on some of my expeditions and got to know Sheera and my family.

Howard was the one who told me that my brother Jack had been killed in action by the Karens at the battle in Maymyo in 1949. Jack was stationed at Maymyo with the Burmese engineers. There were hardly any Burmese army there, so the local engineers had to fight. He had a Bible in his pocket where the bullet struck, protecting his heart, but his head was blown off. Some of our friends were fighting with him and some of our Karen friends were fighting against him. My family was devastated by his death. He left behind a wife and child.

Four of the Hodgson sons were in the military, but on opposite sides of the conflict. People who knew that my brothers were in the Burmese military and I in the Karen army used to say, "The brothers are on opposite sides fighting each other." To me, the Burmese army was the enemy. If my brothers put on the enemy uniform, they were the enemy; if they took off the uniform, however, they were no longer the enemy—they were my brothers.

It was normal in my family to join the military. I just joined the rebel army. While they went by train around the country, I went by foot. They lived in towns and cities and I went into the jungle—for half a century.

When I became a brigadier, one of my relatives asked my sister about me when he visited her in Rangoon. He thought I would do something out of the way like this. But now I was a brigadier general, I was no more a rascal.

The 88 Generation Students Come to Kawthoolei

In 1988 the Burmese government was in reverse gear, not going forward but going from bad to worse. If democracy came, it meant an end to the Burmese Way to Socialism. During the 1970s and 1980s the economy had deteriorated. The people living in Karen State suffered some effects of the poor economy, but not as bad as the rest of Burma. This was because we could buy goods from Thailand. The Burmese government owned all the land in Burma; people would work the land, and then sell the produce overseas to maintain the army. With no income, survival was by hook or by crook. People didn't have enough to eat. If the government hadn't sold our rice overseas, there would have been enough food for the local people. Burmese socialism tried to teach us that without the army everyone would suffer. But it was because of the army that everyone was suffering. They really didn't care for the general population.

When the 1988 demonstrations happened, we were impressed by how people were prepared to give up their lives for democracy.[3] When the protests started, General Ne Win said on the radio that the army had guns and live rounds and warned the protestors that his troops wouldn't hesitate to shoot. The protestors ignored his threat—and the army responded by firing live rounds at them.

My staff went to Hpa-An to gather intelligence on what was happening as more and more students began fleeing Rangoon. They didn't want to be ruled by the military regime and live under Burmese socialism anymore. They wanted democracy, and the National League for Democracy (NLD) emerged.[4]

Some of the students wanted to fight like us because the military would not listen to them. They joined us and asked us for weapons. They also asked other ethnic groups fighting the military to cooperate with them. I was surprised when all the students in 1988 came to Karen State to fight. Some of these students who joined us became good soldiers, but others had rarely fought. Some students who couldn't rough it went back.

The Democratic Alliance of Burma (DAB) was formed at Manerplaw.[5] In addition to most of the members of the National Democratic Front (NDF), it included a dozen new rebel organizations, such as the All Burma Students Democratic Front (ABSDF).[6]

---

3. The nationwide uprising on August 8, 1988, (also known as the four 8s or 8888) was the biggest urban protest against the military junta since the 1970s, and it began as a series of student-led protests. Many of the "88 Generation" students were prodemocracy activists who took part in the uprising; many were subsequently killed or imprisoned in repression after the SLORC assumed power.

4. The National League for Democracy (NLD) was founded on September 27, 1988, and became the main democratic opposition in Burma. The party won 392 of the 485 parliamentary seats in the 1990 general election, but the new military junta of the SLORC refused to recognize the result and transfer state power. After political restrictions were reduced, the NLD won the 2015 general election a quarter of a century later and assumed government office in March 2016.

5. The Democratic Alliance of Burma (DAB) was a broad-based alliance of ethnic minority forces and Burman democracy opposition groups to the junta. The alliance was formed on November 5, 1988, in the aftermath of the uprising. The founding members included the All Burma Students Democratic Front, the New Mon State Party, the Karen National Union, and twenty other anti-junta groups.

6. The National Democratic Front was formed in 1976 as an alliance of nine ethnic political parties and organizations that promoted federalism and aimed to present a coherent (noncommunist) political front against the central government. By the late 1980s the NDF headquarters housed representatives from the KNU, the Arakan Liberation Party (ALP), the Chin National Front (CNF), the Kachin Independence Organization (KIO), the Karenni National Progressive Party (KNPP), the New Mon State Party (NMSP), the Pa-O National Organization (PNO), the Shan State Progress Party (SSPP), and several other parties, together with their corresponding armies. It became virtually defunct in the 1990s when several member organizations signed ceasefire agreements with the State Law and Order

In September 1988, in the wake of the prodemocracy uprising in Rangoon and other towns, the Burmese army conducted another coup, crushed the uprising, and established the State Law and Order Restoration Council (SLORC) under the leadership of Senior General Saw Maung.[7] When Ne Win retired, we didn't feel anything different because it didn't matter who was in power. The rulers still maintained the same strategy. After the 1988 coup, once again nothing changed for the Karen people or the Karen army.

They put a comedian in prison for cracking a joke about the government. He said that when General Saw Maung was a divisional commander and went from one division to another, his real name was Maung Khway, meaning little dog. When he was transferred to Kachin State, he was called Duwa Maung Khway. *Duwa* is a respectful name for men in Kachin State. In Arakan, they called him Khaing Maung Khway out of similar respect. When he came to Karen State, they were going to call him Saw Maung Khway, because *Saw* is a Karen term for Mr. They were in the middle of saying his name on the radio, when the broadcast was interrupted by the announcement that the army had taken power. The announcer dared not call him *Khway*, which means dog in Burmese, so he became known as Saw Maung and lost the name Khway.

Restoration Council government. The All Burma Students Democratic Front (ABSDF) is an armed group formed by student activists who fled to the border areas after the military takeover in 1988.

7. In 1997, the SLORC was renamed the State Peace and Development Council (SPDC). The SPDC was officially dissolved in 2011, giving way to quasi-civilian rule again. But, under the new 2008 constitution, the armed forces continue to control three ministries and a quarter of all seats in parliament.

PSYCHOLOGICAL WARFARE

In the early 1990s Manerplaw was the target of major SLORC offensives; by 1992 these offensives involved more than ten thousand troops. However, the KNLA had managed a successful defense, taking advantage of their battle tactics and the SLORC's lack of familiarity with the area.

Sleeping Dog Hill was close to Manerplaw. If the enemy were to capture it, they could bombard Manerplaw from there. We needed to hold the hill so they couldn't shell Manerplaw. It was like a delayed reaction. The enemy wanted it, so we knew we had to protect it, and posted our soldiers there. There were three battles for this hill, all three of which the Karens won, but I wasn't involved in any of them.

At the time, the Karen army was quite satisfied with the number of soldiers they had because if they had more soldiers, they would need more money to feed them. The KNLA normally recruited volunteers. Some soldiers on home leave liked to tell war stories, which inspired some boys to enlist because they wanted to become soldiers too.

In 1992, though, I was informed by some villagers of Hlaingbwe township in Hpa-An district that some of our military officers had been involved in some serious misdemeanors against the local civilian Karen population that had caused great unhappiness among the people. The villagers were upset because the KNLA officers were forcibly recruiting troops. Two KNLA officers, Lieutenant Charles and San Lom Gyi, were recruiting from two different units but they were behaving like the Burmese army. San Lom Gyi was known as "Mr. Duck" because at every village he went to, he demanded villagers cook a fresh duck for him. The villagers dared not report it so they just groaned quietly. You could make out from the way they were acting that they were upset, even though they didn't say anything.

The two Karen recruiters said to the Karen villagers, "Why do you give your children to the Burmese army when we are different races? They are fighting Karens. Why must your children serve them? Why don't you give your children to us also? We are Karens." The two then pushed the villagers to give them a certain number of recruits too, so the villagers started contributing soldiers to both sides of the conflict. Families became divided and battle information was shared. Some tried to get their children back, and were angry that they had to pay off the recruiting officers to retrieve their children. The Karen officers were doing something very wrong, just like the Burmese army. In spite of being ordered not to do this, they did it, to my dismay.

I was angry and upset when I heard what the two officers were doing, but above all I was angry because they were imitating the Burmese. If they were forcibly recruiting, they were just as bad as the Burmese and the "water" that was the Karen people would "dry up."

This put me at the center of what was to become a very serious situation inside the KNU. When it started, we were hearing stories and my staff went to investigate. Even though there was a problem, we didn't send in the authorities because some people, including Bo Mya, were friendly with the two officers. Some of us didn't want to raise problems or be troublemakers. We didn't tell Bo Mya because we also knew he would probably believe the two officers over us and the official reports. So we told the battalion commanders and left them to deal with it. After we investigated, though, I don't think they stopped doing it. They were just more discreet.

The incident had big consequences. The people's resentment of the misconduct of these officers, and the failure of their leaders to remove them or take action against them, boiled up again in 1994, when Buddhist monks and the Karen Buddhist community expressed their dissatisfaction. A Karen Buddhist monk named U Thuzana, based in Myaing Gyi Ngu village, was favored by the Burmese chief of military intelligence at the time, Lieutenant General Khin Nyunt, who would go by helicopter to visit the monk and take him presents.[1]

---

1. U Thuzana tapped into resentment among Buddhist Karen soldiers in the KNLA toward the wealthier and more educated Christian Karen leadership of the KNLA. He prophesized that by building fifty pagodas, peace would come for the Karens (Gravers 2001). His followers—approximately two thousand Karen families living around his monastery and following his teachings—believed that he had supernatural powers (Ibid.). Subsequently, senior KNU officers privately admitted that the problems of alienation in local communities that had suffered from years of unending conflict went

It was like bribery. Khin Nyunt told the monk that the Christian Karens were oppressing Buddhist Karens. He said the Burmese would support him to build new pagodas at strategic points, places that had plenty of water or were good for military maneuvers. Khin Nyunt said he could find supplies like cement and bricks to build the pagodas.

The KNLA would not allow them to build the pagodas there because they were strategically important for our operations and our strategic terrain. We explained to the monk we couldn't allow him to build them yet because we were still fighting and it was still a battlefield. We asked the monks to stay quiet for now.

The monk told General Khin Nyunt what we had said, and the general offered to clear the area if the monks wished them to. He said there would be no more Manerplaw, so the monks could build as many pagodas as they wanted. At first the monk said he didn't support the idea, but as time went on he began to like it more and more.

U Thuzana started talking and dividing Christians and Buddhists. He said that the Buddhist Karens were oppressed by the Christian Karens, who built churches but not Buddhists monasteries. He had a lot of support for his views—lots of young Buddhist Karen civilians had joined the revolution, and he stirred up their parents to call back their children. He told them that their children would all become Christians and wouldn't listen to their parents anymore. The parents grew alarmed and wanted their children back.

At first, the Buddhists didn't complain about their Christian compatriots, but they started to do so when Khin Nyunt's propaganda influenced Buddhist soldiers. It's called a "whispering campaign" in intelligence. They were whispering negative things about Christians. They were saying the Christians liked to boss everyone around.

I first heard the whispers a few months before the problem started. I didn't tell Bo Mya because at that time it wasn't so serious, and I thought it would be best if he heard for himself. I thought if I told him, he'd investigate further, and it could actually get worse. I only told him about it when he asked. A few weeks later, he heard for himself. Bo Mya was friendly with everybody and he listened to whoever gave him information. That's why you had to be careful what you reported to him because he believed everybody until he knew they

---

deeper than simply the behavior of a few KNLA commanders. A sense of local discrimination against Buddhists came to undermine support for the KNU, including among non-Buddhists. For a detailed analysis of these events, see Gravers 2018. Lieutenant General Khin Nyunt was the head of Myanmar's Military Intelligence and masterminded the military's ceasefire policies beginning in 1989. He was a high-ranking officer in the SLORC and SPDC and briefly became prime minister in 2003 before being placed under house arrest in 2004.

were lying and then he would never trust them again. Some people just go and tell him this and that, especially old ladies. We called reports from old ladies "kitchen news."

Knowing people were dissatisfied with the recruiting, Khin Nyunt tried to connect the forced recruitment of local villagers by the two KNLA officers to the religious issue being whispered about. This only made the situation worse. Unfortunately we didn't take action at once because we thought that if we took action against U Thuzana it would cause a division sooner.

We had to go slowly. We knew what was going on, as I was getting reports about what this monk was doing. I did what I could; I kept working normally because everyone was watching what information we were collecting and sending. I tried to stop the problem from getting worse.

In November 1994, Bo Mya called for a meeting to settle the issues between the Buddhist and the Christian Karens. I was at the meeting. We invited everyone, including some monks and Christians. Bo Mya wanted to settle it face to face with U Thuzana, but he didn't come. He didn't come because he was guilty; maybe he was afraid that if he came, he might be arrested. Bwe Paw said he didn't come because he was guilty of orchestrating the whole thing, that if his conscience was clear he would have come. One of the monks started crying, saying that this will lead to Karens fighting Karens. Everyone was upset.

Bo Mya said that since the majority of monks were here the meeting could go ahead without U Thuzana; it was not necessary to have another meeting for just one person. Bo Mya asked everyone to speak frankly and get it out in the open to avoid misunderstanding and find the mistakes that needed correcting.

They talked about how it wasn't like this before, how people didn't talk about religion. Before, Christian soldiers sometimes went to the Burmese monastery on special days for dances and feasts while Buddhists attended Christmas celebrations, even singing carols although they were not Christian. Nobody was bothered, but now the situation was creating problems.

The majority of people wanted everything to be peaceful. Bo Mya told them to go back and say all of this to U Thuzana. "Whatever you do," he said, "you must be very careful because the Burmese will use this against us." I just kept my mouth shut—we were trying to avoid a split.

After the meeting, everything got worse. Nobody wanted the situation to turn out how it did; one monk had already cried. We knew the split was coming and we couldn't stop it.

U Thuzana got arms and brought them in by the Moei and Salween rivers to his monastery. The monk told all the Buddhists to join him, otherwise they would end up floating in the Salween River: "Bo Mya will kill all of you if you don't come, so come, even at the last minute, hurry!"

Some of our Buddhist soldiers went, but there were many who didn't take any notice and stayed with us; even some of those close to the monk whose parents asked them to come back didn't go back. There were no reprisals against those Buddhists who stayed. We knew that Khin Nyunt was behind it.

None of my Buddhist staff left. They could judge for themselves that it was psychological warfare; in their training they had learned about it and what to do when the enemy used it. They were taught how to judge situations like this.

When the Buddhist soldiers left, I thought to myself, "One day they'll realize what happened, but it will be too late because they will have been disarmed."

Religious people have no mind for politics. It's a weak point that we cannot train them in. They know that they are patriots—the soldiers and the people—because they are Karens. From birth they only know that they are Karen so they must defend the Karens. But if somebody can tell them twisted stories the way Khin Nyunt did, they can easily fall into his pocket.

I am careful when I talk about Christianity with the Karens because there are many religions among Karens, and it is not good to mix up religion with politics—it can become very complicated. For me, the military leadership can be Muslim, Christian, or Buddhist. Religion and the military must be kept separate.

Before U Thuzana got involved, we weren't worried about a split in the Karen army. We thought it was possible that the Buddhists could split but that it would be a minority. Some other monks didn't like the idea of a split and told U Thuzana that he was a monk, not a politician, so he shouldn't poke his nose in political affairs. Since he was a monk, he should behave like a monk.

By early December 1994, some Buddhist KNLA troops were in open revolt against the KNU. On December 21, they formed the Democratic Karen Buddhist Army (DKBA). There were skirmishes between the KNLA and DKBA soldiers, but the first battle was at Manerplaw.

Radio monitoring gave the SLORC government a virtually complete picture of both the political and the military dimensions of the DKBA rebellion. At the operational level, the human intelligence the SLORC obtained from the DKBA was a decisive factor in the capture of Manerplaw.

When the Burmese army started operations against the Karens, the Buddhist Karens acted as guides and then interpreters because the Burmese soldiers could not speak Karen. Before, when the Burmese army had come to Karen areas, all the villagers deserted their villages, so the army could not get guides. DKBA soldiers were attached to each Burmese unit to guide them. When the fighting started, the DKBA soldiers fought their former KNLA comrades.

When Karens were fighting Karens, I didn't feel anything because I knew the DKBA wouldn't last long; it was like they were putting a scorpion or snake in their pocket. I think Bo Mya thought that if a Burmese soldier was on our side, he's a Karen. If a Karen soldier is on the Burmese side, he is a Burman.

I think both sides didn't want to shoot Karens, but in the battlefield you cannot select who is who, you have to shoot the enemy. When they attacked, the Burmese soldiers and DKBA were all mixed up, so you couldn't tell who was Burmese and who was Karen. Whoever shot at you, you had to shoot back. But the Burmese and the DKBA didn't need to choose because everyone they were shooting at was Karen.

At that time no one was happy because Karens were on both sides, the Karen people were divided, and they were forced to fight each other. The majority of the Karen population didn't like the idea of Karens fighting each other and being separated, but we could not avoid it.

By 1995 the settlement at Manerplaw consisted of the KNU and KNLA headquarters, the ABSDF camp and communication center, and the NDF and DAB communications centers. Manerplaw was generally regarded as "virtually impregnable" because of the surrounding mountainous terrain.

The SLORC campaign to capture Manerplaw in January 1995 involved at least ten thousand SLORC troops, from the Twenty-Second, Thirty-Third, Forty-Fourth, and Sixty-Sixth light infantry divisions. However, the SLORC victory was due less to its overwhelming numerical superiority over the KNLA than to the treachery of the DKBA troops, who guided the SLORC forces through the camp's formidable defenses. The Burmese army's campaign was commanded by Lieutenant General Maung Hla, who had been in charge of the 1992 offensive on Manerplaw and was based in Hpa-An.

The KNLA command structure was poorly organized for the defense of Manerplaw. Lieutenant Colonel Law Wadi was the head of the KNLA operational department at the GHQ. On February 4, 1995, after a month of sporadic fighting, Manerplaw was captured. Strategically the fall of Manerplaw was bad for the Karens because it was their headquarters, but leaders have to take responsibility for everything, the good and bad.

I was in Manerplaw while the enemy was preparing to attack. We knew the enemy would attack because a major operation was clearly being prepared. They could not come secretly; they had to come openly and they had to use force. Before they actually attacked, I was sent to Wangkha to support the Seventh Brigade and 101 Special Battalion there. There were so many elders at Manerplaw, but we needed some elders in Wangkha, so they sent me.

That was the last time I saw Manerplaw. I couldn't take anything with me. I had my staff with me, and they also couldn't take anything. We only took our weapons and personal belongings. All my documents and photos were left behind in one of the villagers' huts.

Other officers—those who were at Manerplaw—could move their families who were living in Htoo Wah Lu and other nearby villages. As for me, I was somewhere else, so Sheera had to stay until the last minute. But at the last minute, she couldn't do anything. As the battle began she took some rice and blankets and fled to the jungle in Thailand. It was December, so it was very cold. Because I wasn't near, I couldn't arrange anything for her. Although she was sixty-two years old, she had to escape by walking out through the jungle.

I didn't feel anything when the enemy captured Manerplaw because the whole time it was always like hide and seek. Our officers had to burn everything so many times and had to evacuate so many times. Sometimes we did not even have enough time to evacuate. Sometimes we just had to run. I was quite used to it.

Some old Christian ladies said the fall of Manerplaw was Bo Mya's fault because he was a Christian and he allowed a Buddhist monastery to be built in Manerplaw. The committee members who were Christians had to go and carry bricks to build the pagoda, so God saw and disapproved of it. Since Bo Mya ordered it, it was his fault. It was Bo Mya's problem because he was a Christian building idols.

At the time Manerplaw fell, I was a central committee member in the KNU. Two weeks later Padoh Ba Thin, the KNU general secretary, and I moved to Hti Nuh area, attached to General Bo Mya. The vice chief of staff Tamlar Baw asked us to stay close to give him advice. Later, when Bo Mya had some more people around him, he asked me to stay with the Sixth Brigade at Palu and guard the custom gate.

The same day I got there the enemy captured Palu. Before the gate fell, the Thai Third Army Commander asked who was commanding on the Karen side and he was told only Major Mu Tu and me; although I hadn't arrived yet, they knew I was coming. The Thai army commander said, "Oh don't worry. Both of them are good fighters." But when I finally arrived, that same day it fell. I was too late by a few hours. The enemy was quicker than me.

Even though Manerplaw fell, I never felt that we would lose the revolution. Previously, we used to hold towns like Taungoo and Pegu and then we lost them. Nothing happened because in the strategy of active defense or guerrilla warfare, you may lose your position but still maintain the support of the people. You can lose your position, you can lose battles, but you must not lose the support of the masses and you must not lose the war.

When the Burmese wanted to conduct an operation in an area, they had peace talks with ethnic groups in nearby areas. If they wanted to attack the Kachins they had peace talks with the Karens, so the Burmese troops could withdraw from the Karen area in order to attack the Kachin area.

After Manerplaw fell, my staff also could not locate their families. I gave them leave to do so. One of my staff, Lieutenant Saw Loh, was captured by the enemy at Khler Thay Lu. A week later, another of my staff, Corporal Timothy went to Mu Wah Kwi village, not far from Khler Thay Lu, to try to locate his family. He also was captured. He was interrogated concerning my whereabouts and tortured to death. The refugee camp there was destroyed. Five days later, another two of my staff, Hpa Di and Hpa Lah, went to Baw Naw refugee camp also trying to locate their families. These two were also captured and interrogated. They gave no information so they were tortured and the refugee camp was destroyed.

I think they were courageous and stubborn. The Burmese were asking about my movements and my plans. Because they were my staff, they must have known what I was doing. I think they kept their mouths shut. I felt sorry when I found out they died. But that is war; you cannot avoid it.

The rest of my staff and I could not stay in the Hlaingbwe area any longer, so we moved southwards to the Kanelay area where the Sixth Brigade was. Our intelligence was telling us the enemy was determined to try and capture KNU leaders, including me, and would continue raids and attacks on refugee camps until we were found.

I think that I was also targeted by the DKBA because some of those who had deserted from the KNU were criminals whom I'd had responsibility for disciplining as part of my duty. I was often selected to act as a head of a judicial committee to deal with such wrongdoers, and some of these may have harbored ill feelings toward me. This means they were willing to carry out the orders of their SLORC commanders who were anxious to capture senior members of the KNLA and KNU.

In April 1995, the KNU called an emergency meeting, but owing to enemy activity in Hti Nuh area the meeting was postponed and continued at Kanelay. After the meeting, my staff and I moved to Waw Lei Khi with Padoh San Lin.

The Sixteenth Battalion commander under the KNLA Sixth Brigade was Thu Mu Hai, who was responsible for security in the west of that territory, but instead of resisting the enemy; he surrendered with many of his troops. When he surrendered, we couldn't stay anywhere because the friends of the enemy were everywhere. We were stuck between the Burmese army and the Thai army in the forests along the border. We could not openly go to Thailand and we could not stay in Burma.

Before, we used to cooperate with Thai intelligence and share our information. They gave us a special permit from their headquarters so we could go anywhere in Thailand. If there was any question about the permit, then there was a phone number to call. The Thai border patrol police's duty was to monitor security measures on the border. Now, to collect information, they hunted us everywhere, wanting to know whether our soldiers had gone across and hid in the jungle when they didn't find them in the refugee camps.

We stayed separated from the other soldiers. The Thai were hunting all around us. They came across six or seven of us who had stayed separate. I told them that I had come there on duty, which was to go around their border. They asked if the Thai authorities knew that I had duties along this border, and I showed them the permit. They apologized and didn't ask any further questions. They asked, "Why don't you stay in the village at the headman's house or something? Why stay in the jungle?" I replied that I didn't want to bother people and I didn't want people to know that we were going around because we were doing this for border security for both sides. If we stayed in the village we were exposing ourselves. We wanted to stay hidden. After that, nobody questioned us anymore.

Some of our soldiers and their families came across the border and then contacted someone in Mae Sot in Thailand via radio or a message given to another person to come and fetch them. We had no one to fetch us. I asked those who came to fetch the other people if I could go with them. They said that they couldn't because of the checkpoints, and they warned that the checkpoints were strict now, especially when military operations were going on. I said, "No, I can keep quiet. You can talk with the checkpoint guards and I'll stay in the car. I won't speak." "No, no!" they cried, "We'll get into trouble because of you!" I didn't tell them I had a permit.

In Mae Sot, a Thai colonel asked my son Ler Paw where I was. He told him I was in the Sixth Brigade Area. The colonel asked why I didn't come to Mae Sot. My son answered, "It's very hard to come because all the checkpoints are strict." Then the Thai colonel sent his staff to come and meet me with their military permit. They met me, and on the way to Mae Sot I saw those who had refused to take me along. They were checked and delayed. I said to my escort, "Please tell them I have no permission to talk. I said I wouldn't speak."

I met the intelligence officer in Mae Sot and we discussed the situation. The Thai wanted to know how much information I had about the Thai troops and our troops, our location and the Burmese location. The Thai army was friendly with the Karen army, but if there were military operations they wouldn't be friends anymore because they were quite afraid of the Burmese and what they would do if the Thai were seen to be our friends.

I saw Sheera again in Mae Sot. We had both gone through hardships in our separate lives. Since she had fled Manerplaw, Sheera had been living in different refugee camps and continuing her work as General Secretary of the Karen Women's Organisation. It was quite tough for her, but it was just as tough for me. I could not worry about just one person; I had to worry about the whole country.

I applied for and was granted extended leave (known as long leave) from the KNLA. I had originally applied to retire when I was 60 years old, in 1990, because I said I could not do anything more and it was time for younger generations to take over. But Bo Mya and the others kept telling me to wait, to hold on.

At first, we said we'd fight a "father to son" war. In such a war, the father serves in the revolution. When he retires, he cannot do anything more so his son fights, thereby continuing his father's war. But because the father to son war hasn't finished yet, it will go on to become a "father to grandson" war.

When I went on leave, my second in command, Colonel Ho Paw, took over from me. I only told General Shwe Hser that I was going to Bangkok where I would contact the Australian Embassy and apply to relocate to Perth where my brother was living. He didn't say anything because he knew I was taking a long leave to move into retirement. If I had retired in Thailand or near the border, I wouldn't really retire because I would be in the same place. He knew that if I retired in Australia, I would not come back.

I never officially retired from the KNLA. I'm still officially on leave. My former colleagues still ask me if I have completed my long leave yet.

LIFE AFTER THE REVOLUTION

After arriving in Mae Sot, we lived in Mae La refugee camp (known as Bae Klaw refugee camp in Karen). There were about twenty-five thousand people living there at that time. We stayed with my son Saw Ler Paw, his wife Karen, and their young son Ernest.

In August 1997, Thai intelligence took my family and me to Bangkok, where we stayed in an apartment in the Maneeloy Burmese Student Center that had been set up for democracy refugees who had fled Burma after the suppression of the 1988 protests. We applied for and were granted UNHCR refugee status, and that gave us some money for rent and food.

My brother Howard applied to sponsor us to come to Australia. We were old and didn't have identity documents, so we waited in Bangkok for over a year for the Australian embassy to respond to our request for resettlement.

We were very bored in Bangkok. Every day we read anything to pass the time. We could not go outside because immigration police were everywhere tracking down refugees and those who had come to work illegally. When refugees were caught breaking the law, the Thais would send them back to the border.

After applying to the UNHCR, we were given ID numbers and classified as Persons of Concern, so if we were arrested, the UN would have to go and redeem us. The UN staff would have to come see if they recognized you, and if they did, they would collect you. You would not be happy when this happened because you were arrested, even though you were later released. If you are arrested, it hurts your pride. Fortunately, I was never caught by immigration.

When I was living in Bangkok, Bo Mya came to ask me to go back to the army. He was angry when he found out that I had been granted long leave and scolded those who granted it to me. That was why I didn't tell him at the time; I knew he would say no. He saw my friends in Bangkok, who told him that they only saw me when I went out. They didn't know my location. But they had a telephone number for me, so if he wanted to speak to me, he could ring me.

He rang me and asked, "Why did you leave? Is there anything that hurt your feelings?" I said, "Nothing." He asked, "Is there anything that dissatisfied you?" I said, "Nothing." "Why then?" he asked again.

I told him that I had requested to retire since I turned sixty years old, yet he kept saying wait, wait. Slowly I had become a burden on the army. At the front line they could not use me because at night I had to use a flashlight. The soldiers knew how to move in the dark, but I could not. I could not march like I could in younger days because I walked very slowly. Just for my sake the whole column had to move at my speed—and if I walked only three miles, the column could only walk three miles. I'd had enough already of staying behind at headquarters. I didn't want to be a burden on the army, I told him.

He said, "Yes, but your mouth is still OK, and you can still speak and advise." I replied that things were changing very quickly and it's not like in our days. When we started our revolution in Insein we only had a rifle and five rounds of ammo, but nowadays our soldiers are using rocket launchers and they are all up to date. When we were able-bodied we could see the enemy, but with five rounds if you were not sure, you dared not fire because then you would only have four rounds left. We waited until we were just about a stone's throw away before we would shoot. Nowadays we don't see each other but our arms can reach the enemy, so whether you can see the enemy or not, you shoot. Weapons are so advanced today, so I cannot advise the frontline soldiers.

"When we talk about having only a rifle and five bullets each, the younger soldiers cannot believe us." I continued. "How do you fight with only five bullets? If you talk about up-to-date weapons they may be interested, but they wouldn't be interested in fifty-year-old weapons. There is a vast difference, a big generation gap. If they want to know about rifles and bullets they can ask me, and I will tell them, but I won't go around lecturing them. If you were in my place, you'd do the same thing."

I told him that since I was now ten years older than I was when I requested to retire, I wanted to be quiet. I could not retire in Burma or at the border because I would not be able to retire in peace. I could not retire in Thailand because we were not Thai citizens and it was very difficult for us to stay here. I had applied to UNHCR to stay far away where my siblings are and where there is no more war.

I told him that I had done enough for the Karen people and I had done enough for myself, but I hadn't done anything for God. If I stayed far away, I could attend church every weekend and go to Bible study every week. I could occupy my mind with religion and forget about the past. "I think I have done my duty," I said.

Bo Mya thought it over and he gave a big sigh. "All right," he said, "I won't stop you and I think that's a very good idea. But don't forget your people because you have stayed together with them and you know their situation. Even if you get to the country with milk and honey flowing, don't forget those people still suffering. Remember them." I said, "Yes." He didn't say anything else and hung up the phone.

Sheera was close friends with Bo Mya's wife, Lah Po. She was Sheera's chairperson at the Karen Women's Organization. I think Lah Po didn't want Sheera to go and asked her husband to get me to go back so Sheera would also come back.

That was the last time I spoke to Bo Mya. He died in 2006. His son came to visit us in Australia because his mother told him that if he went to Australia he should go and see Sheera. She said she wanted something from Sheera to remember her by, so Sheera bought her a wristwatch and wrote her a letter.

Coming to Australia

When we arrived in Australia all the relatives—almost everybody—came to the airport. The youngest generation had only heard about me and wanted to see me, for after Burma's independence and the beginning of the revolution many of my family members went to other countries. Here in Australia, I saw my sister Violet, who had also moved to Perth with her children after her husband's death in Rangoon. When she saw me again after five decades, she said that I now looked like our father. I saw her for one month exactly and then she died. I was so glad to see her again but sad because we only had one month together.

A few years later in 2005, I went to the United States to visit Maureen and her husband before going to Montreal to see my eldest sister Margaret. When I met her again, I didn't know whether to cry, laugh, or what. I thought: if she cries, I will cry. But she also thought: if I cry, she will cry. So, I think, nobody cried. Out of the family, Margaret loved me the most. When I was young, I stayed with her the most out of everyone in our family and she was very fond of me.

When I went to Canada my two nieces, my half-sister Florence's children who live in the UK, came to visit Margaret too. When we met them we hugged and we all cried. Florence had immigrated with her family to the UK but had passed away years earlier.

My sisters Fanny and Edna stayed in Rangoon. My sisters never wanted to leave Burma and it wasn't until 2014 that I saw Edna again in Thailand. She told me then what had happened that day many decades earlier in Insein when the revolution began and our family was evacuated. She said that the British told everyone to get on a big truck. Edna was busy trying to find all her siblings and Florence's children and get them on the truck. They filled up the truck, but my sisters were looking for the lost sheep who had disappeared—me. An Anglo-Burmese embassy staffer yelled that if we didn't leave now, the Burmese would start shooting at us, since there was only five minutes left of the ceasefire. My oldest sister Edna cried that she was not going without her brother.

She felt guilty. She supported the Karen cause and believed that she had put it into my head to join the Karen Revolution. She was terrified that if I joined the revolution I wouldn't come back, or I would come back without a limb. Finally, Florence coaxed Edna to get on the truck. She still looked for me as the truck drove away.

All the decades since, she had blamed herself because she was the eldest sibling in Insein and therefore in charge of the younger ones. When we met again, sixty-five years later, she told me that to see me was like the song "Amazing Grace." I told her that now she didn't have to worry because Burmese bullets could not reach Australia. Edna used to say to her children and grandchildren that they had to listen to her because she lost her younger brother during the civil war when he didn't listen to her.

I told her it was God's plan, not our plan, that I stayed behind in Insein. She told me that now she could see it was God's plan that I didn't go with them that day. She said that there were Burmese troops at the checkpoint checking everyone on the trucks. The trucks were filled with women, children, and the elderly. They were taking down any able-bodied men from the trucks and taking them away. If I had been there, they probably would have forced me off the truck and taken me away. She was relieved because all this time she had been blaming herself.

Howard later told me that when they got to the military checkpoint, Wilbur was waiting for them in his Burmese army uniform with his gun by his side. Once he told the soldiers at the checkpoint that they were his family, they stopped harassing them. Wilbur then took them to my father in Rangoon.

The family was afraid that the Burmese would interrogate them about my joining the revolution so they made up a cover story to explain what happened. They said that I had been asked to go out and buy fish sauce, but I got caught up in the fighting and never came home. They made it sound like I accidently joined the revolution. That was what they told their children had happened to me and after many years it became family legend.

The whole time I was in the revolution, my family lived with the worry that I would be killed and never knew if I was dead or alive. They were scared to talk about me in case the enemy found out. They didn't dare tell anyone outside the family that I was in the revolution. My sister Edna was married to a Karen officer who served in the Burmese navy, and he had been on the navy boats shelling us in Insein. He was a noble and honest man, so my sister feared that if she told him about me he would feel compelled to tell his superiors. She lived for decades never telling him, and her husband died not knowing about me. The burden and worry my family carried was great.

A year after I saw Edna in Chiang Mai, she passed away. I'm grateful that she came to Thailand so I could see her one last time and she could meet Sheera. My relatives said that after seeing me one last time, a burden was lifted, and she could finally be at peace.

After sixty years I spoke to my former fiancée Baby again through the computer set up by our nieces. She didn't speak at all; only her nieces spoke. She never forgave me for not coming back for her when the revolution began. She had heard through others that I had joined the revolution, but she waited for me anyway. Eventually she married a Burmese doctor, just like she had predicted that night in Rangoon back in 1949.

Her sister married my boss General Tamlar Baw. When we visited him in Thailand in 2014, Baby came to the house to see her sister. She just stared at me and didn't say anything. I think she must have been cursing me.

Settling in Perth

We settled in the working-class suburb of Gosnells in the south of Perth. Howard, now a pastor, lives nearby with his family. When we first came to Australia, we were not so happy because everything was very different—culture, language, and way of life.

After we arrived we started to learn English at a vocational college in Perth. During the first year, I didn't like it much because I thought I was too old to study. Everybody had to attend classes, including our children and grandchildren, and it was so awkward to study with your grandchildren. When we spoke with the students and teachers, they didn't understand us and we didn't understand them.

During the revolution, all my English was left behind. When I started school in Australia it was like revision for me, and the language came back to me. Our teachers were surprised with me. This old man, they thought, has a very good knowledge of the English language. They did not know my story; I only told them that I had been a locomotive engineer. They thought I was starting from scratch. Soon, I was the brightest in the class, especially in writing.

But as for me, I try to be modest. Modesty and humility are important in Karen culture, and most Karens are modest. Sometimes they know something, but say that they don't know. For instance, you can play the piano, but you don't admit it unless you are asked.

When I came to Australia I learned more about Christianity. Before I came to Australia, I used to drink, smoke, and chew betel nut. I prayed that one day by hook or by crook I would stop drinking and smoking. Every year I made a resolution to stop but I never succeeded.

When I attended English classes I had no time to drink, chew, or smoke. When I came home, I had all my homework to do, so I just lost interest in it. After a few weeks I thought, I can stop, and automatically I stopped. When my friends offered me a drink, I said, "Sorry, I don't want to start all over again." Everyone was surprised, as it was very rare to see someone drop all his habits at once because it's so hard to drop bad habits one at a time.

At the same time, I started to delve into Bible study. As I learned more about Christianity, I became born again and became more serious about church and the Bible. Before, all I knew was to go to church and listen to the pastor, but my thoughts were elsewhere. I just went for the sake of going and prayed because I had to pray. I didn't connect the dots. But when I got to Australia, I could ask questions and read the Bible every day. It made more sense now and all came together. Before my prayers were superficial, now I have faith when I pray; now I believe that God will answer my prayer.

There is little difference between my life before and after I was born again. At first, it was quite hard because I wasn't used to religious life. Sometimes at a prayer meeting when the pastor asked us to say grace, I would ask Sheera to do it. I was not used to it because my life had been personal prayer only, not in a group or in public.

Adjusting to Civilian Life

When I retired, I took off my uniform and I had to get used to the fact that I was no longer a soldier. I had become a civilian. When people addressed me by my army rank, I had to correct them and say, "I am no longer in the army; call me uncle or grandfather."

At first, in the daytime I dared not stay home alone. I had never been alone in the army and I wasn't used to it. I was so used to bodyguards; even if I went to the toilet or for a bath, the bodyguard would follow me. But Sheera was used to being alone. She would go out for a little while to see her niece. Over time she stayed out longer and longer. If she went out at night, she would ask our niece to come and stay with me. I made friends with the computer. I would play solitaire and I wouldn't notice time pass because I was concentrating on the game. Now I'm more used to being alone.

People would ask me what I was afraid of. "I'm afraid of ghosts," I'd say. "Have you seen one?" they'd ask. "I've never seen one, but I've been scared of them since I was a little boy," I told them.

During battle, if many people were killed and it got dark before we buried the bodies, we would have to sleep among the Karen and enemy corpses. Over time it became easier to do; like hospital staff we become used to seeing dead bodies.

If I was separated from the other soldiers while retreating, I would have no more companions and I often had to sleep alone. I used to say the Lord's Prayer and recite Psalm 23. Then I could go to sleep. This psalm now hangs on the wall of our home in Australia.

From the beginning, I always thought that when you will die and how you will die is in God's hands. There's nothing I could do. I remember that my father used to say, "Don't worry until worries worry you, don't trouble until trouble troubles you." I used to think to myself, there are many people who have fought many battles and are still alive. There are some recruits who died in their very first battle, while others live to retire, or get shot four or five times but still live.

The older we have become, the easier living has become for us. In Australia we don't have to worry any more. The government helps people in their old age. We are fortunate because we cannot do farming or hard work anymore. Our elderly comrades-in-arms that stayed behind have died one by one. They have had to support themselves; some were undernourished so they didn't last long, others have to keep working to support themselves while their children have to find work in the cities.

During the revolution I was never around for my wife and family. Before, I had my responsibilities and Sheera had hers, so we didn't go out together. Now that we are in Australia we go everywhere together.

We are still very active in our eighties. We attend a multicultural seniors' group once a week and we sometimes go on short vacations with the group. We are always going to prayer meetings and church services. Our grandchildren often stay with us, so we are always busy. I don't worry about my family. I let them worry about themselves. Here in Australia, all of us are safe. And the way of life is not bad.

If I am the eldest at a wedding ceremony, the bride and groom ask me for any wisdom about their new life together. I tell them the advice I once heard from an old man at a wedding: two lovers get married and have three children. One day the wife is not feeling well, so the husband has to cook. When the rice begins to boil, he has to throw away the water. The children quarrel, hit each other, and cry; the younger one is sick and dirties the floor. The wife says, "Look after your children!" He puts the pot down and puts his hands on his hips and says, "The best thing to do is to kill you all." The wife asks, "Then why did you marry me?" He replies: "Because we love each other and wanted to get married. But I didn't expect this!"

You must be patient with your children and wife. There will be difficulties; when you have children, things change, and when you have grandchildren, you change more because they are teaching you. You must be prepared to face difficulties. You must understand this before you face difficulties together.

Now that we are used to living in Australia, we don't miss Burma so much. Previously we missed lots of things. Now it doesn't make any difference where we stay. Nowadays we must not think about the country because we live in the global age. Not that country, not that town, but this whole planet.

One of our friends was a camp commander in Htam Hin refugee camp in Thailand. He's now here in Perth. He wants to go back but his children won't let him. I asked him why he wants to go back. He said he's got nothing to do here because in the morning his grandchildren go to school, and his children go to work. He is alone in the house until the evening when his grandchildren come back from school and his children from work. When he was a camp commander, he had plenty of work to do every hour of every day. Now there is no one around to visit. He lives like the NLD leader Aung San Suu Kyi who was under house arrest for many years.

Some people, when they come to visit Australia, are surprised that there are so many refugees here in Australia. Pastors come to ask for donations to build churches and support Karens in Burma and Karen refugees in Thailand. They

FIGURE 11.   Sheera and Ralph jointly celebrating their birthdays, Perth, 2014

expect the situation for refugees to be the same here as it is in Burma. They are surprised because each refugee here has a good car. In Burma, even officials don't have these cars; they have only Chinese cars. In Australia women also drive, which they couldn't have imagined before arriving here.

In recent years some refugees living in Perth have gone back to visit Burma. If the Burmese government said that they would allow me to go back, if they gave me amnesty, it wouldn't make any difference. I don't want to go back to my hometown, because I would have to introduce myself to everybody. Some may have heard of me, but the majority wouldn't know me. The people we knew are all gone. Only the second and third generations are still around. The first generation may have heard about us from their elders, but they probably didn't tell the second generation.

Many people my age have died from the war, old age—from all sorts of causes. Sometimes, when people from Kawthoolei get our phone number, they phone us and tell me who has gone. I say, "No. Tell me who is still living. Then I'll automatically know who has gone and I'll know who is living." If they tell me only who has gone, the list will be never ending, and I won't get to know who is still living.

I used to write letters to people in Kawthoolei and I'd ask travelers to post or deliver them for me. I'd write that I think about them and ask if they also think about when we were together and how our lives have changed. I'd try to encourage them, so when they get the letter, they'd be happy. These people are in foreign countries, but they still know us. Sometimes we would send them money; I wish I could send more but we only have so much.

When I retired and came to Australia, I told myself to stay out of these revolution matters, because it is no longer my time. So, I try to keep my head cool. But I think the Burmese strategy is still to disarm us. They cannot disarm the ethnic armies by force because everyone will rebel, so they have to twist and turn to try to disarm us. They will try to turn the KNLA into Border Guard Forces like they did with the DKBA and make them come under the Burmese army. They will tell them they don't need heavy weapons like machine guns and mortars to guard the border, and then disarm them.

One DKBA unit deserted because they did not want to come under the command of the Burmese government army.[1] They said, "We are soldiers and we are fighting our own people. If this is the situation, then we will unite with our

---

1. The DKBA breakaway group, known as DKBA Brigade Five, retained a separate identity and agreed to a ceasefire with the government in 2012. The mainstream DKBA transformed into twelve Border Guard Force battalions under Burmese army control in 2010, with a strength of three to four thousand troops. U Thuzana's Myaing Gyi Ngu monastery has remained an important social base among the local population for their activities.

people. Our guns will point to our enemy and we will rest only when peace talks are held." It is like when Hunter Thahmwe went for peace talks in Rangoon in 1963. When he arrived, the newspapers announced that the Karens had surrendered. He was tricked by the Burmans.

Aung San Suu Kyi may be a little better than the previous government, as she was educated in the West and has a broader outlook. The others are frogs in the well and are quite happy with things. She may be different, but she must also have an understanding of the ethnic people.

Some of our friends, when they visit us here, ask me how I see the situation in Burma. I tell them that it will keep dragging on. They say that it has dragged on for over sixty-five years already and ask me what I would do to settle this if I could. I tell them it's very easy, that it only seems hard because the Burmese are afraid of federalism. They want Burma for the Burmans, but if they had federalism they would have to give autonomy to us.

They respond, "But you already have Karen State, Mon State, Shan State, Chin State, Kachin State etc." I tell them that they only mention the ethnic minority states. There's no Burmese state. In federalism there must be a Burmese state. All people in all states must be equal. The states should then join together to form the federal government. Everybody would have the same rights and each state would not be governed by the military. Like in Australia, where each state has their own premier and parliament and together they have the federal government in Canberra.

The Burmans are afraid of federalism because they would have to share equally and give authority to non-Burmans. At the moment the Burmans have 50 percent of the vote and the minorities have the other 50 percent, meaning the minorities cannot beat the Burmans. If they had a Burman state, whether large, narrow, or small, they would have the same rights as the other states. We should all be heard.

Whether Burma will become a federal system will depend on the situation. If the majority, including the Burmans, wants federalism, the Burmese government will have to accept it.

Part 2
THE TEACHER
Naw Sheera's Story

CHILDHOOD

The village I grew up in, Et Et, was paradise. It was a small village, with only sixty to seventy houses, and remote—a two-hour walk to the next village and sixty-six miles from the district capital Tavoy (now Dawei). We were poor. We didn't have many material possessions. We grew all our own food and made everything we needed. We didn't have medicine and we only had a primary school. But there were no burglaries, no thieves, and we weren't afraid of anything. There was no fighting. It was peaceful.

I was born in 1932, the eldest of ten siblings, six of whom died when they were very young. At that time a lot of babies died because there was no hospital for births or for treatable conditions like malaria and diarrhea.

The ones who survived were my brothers Htoo Htoo (the second oldest), Ru Ru (Rupert), and Ten Boy, who was called that because he was the tenth child. I was the only girl in my family and always wanted a sister. But I had many cousins and friends.

My mother's name was Naw Mae Mae and my father's name was Saw Ba Tin. My mother was the eldest of three sisters; I loved my mother and we were close. If anything troubled her she would get angry; otherwise she was cool and calm. My father never scolded or beat me, and I loved him for this. He was not an angry man and he didn't scold his children, only our mother did. Because I was the only girl in my family, my father loved me the most.

When I was a little girl I lived with my grandparents rather than with my parents, as they lived in Et Et village too, but their house was closer to my school than that of my parents, who lived in the fields about an hour's walk away.

My mother was the eldest child in her family, and I the eldest in mine. I was the first grandchild in our whole family, so my grandparents also loved me the most.

My grandparents lived together with their youngest daughter Bwey Paw, my aunt, whose name means snow. She had a baby girl called Pawpre whom my grandmother would look after while her parents went out to work on their farm. My mother had three sisters, but I don't know how many siblings my father had.

In Karen culture, aunts and grandparents treat their nieces, nephews, and grandchildren like their own children. I have the same relationship today with my grandchildren. When my granddaughter comes to stay over, she always wants to sleep in my bed rather than her own. We sleep like Karens, like I did with my grandmother.

My grandfather was a farmer. When I lived with them, my grandfather was old, but he could still work in the fields. At the beginning, I was too young to help my grandmother. I just played. When I was old enough, I learned how to do housework and fetched water from the well for the house.

We loved playing pretend. We would take rice and leaves and pretend to cook fish. Sometimes we would pretend we were in a market, using shells as pretend money, in our own pretend houses and shops.

I had many friends growing up. I would go fishing together with a close friend from the village or we would go into the jungle to look for vegetables together. When we cooked, all of us cooked together.

No one taught me to cook (for real, not pretend); I would just watch my grandmother and copy her. My favorite thing she would cook was rice porridge with chicken, called *tekapor* in Karen. Now I make this for my grandchildren.

My parents and grandparents could all read and write. I started school at the local government school when I was five and studied in the Karen and Burmese languages, but my teacher was Karen. I liked school and loved all my subjects; I was good at schoolwork and the brightest in my class. When the school inspectors came around and started questioning the pupils, I was always the first to raise my hand. They liked that I was quick to answer. When I was at school the teachers asked me what I wanted to be when I grew up and I always said a teacher. I wanted to go to the other villages and teach.

In peaceful times, when I came home from school, I ate a snack and went to chase away the buffalo that would come to eat in our rice paddies with a slingshot.

My parents would come to visit my grandparents and me every Sunday. We would all go together to the village's Baptist church in the school building. My family has been Christian since my grandparents were converted.

When I went to church as a child, I felt happy. I started to learn how to sing songs and tried to study the scripture in Sunday school. One of my schoolteachers taught Sunday school. I can still sing songs like "Ring the Bell in Heaven, God Created Everything."

When I was young, I didn't know anything about Christianity; we just did what the elders told us to do. We went to church because it was tradition, because the whole village went. When I was young I didn't know much about politics either.

The village had a main road that was like a circle around the village, which was the normal layout for Karen villages. The houses were on both sides of the circle, and further out, there was a road to another village. If the neighboring villagers came to visit, they would use that road. Around the outside there were paddy fields.

We had a big garden with lots of space outside our house. We grew mangoes, jackfruit, coconuts, pineapple, durian, and wild lycees. Durian was my favorite fruit. We also raised buffalo, cows, goats, ducks, and chickens, to eat rather than to sell. We would eat them on special occasions and when we had nothing else to eat.

To go to the farms, farmers would have to go through another small village, where people stayed when they were farming nearby fields. It was a about half an hour walk. This was where my parents lived.

Houses in the village had three rooms on one level. We kept farm tools under the house, but also chickens and ducks, especially during the rainy season. My family had enough food because we could go to the forest to hunt animals like birds. We also grew our own vegetables. So we always had enough food.

I learned to raise animals by watching what the older people did and helping them feed and look after the animals. If they had a pig to fatten, they would cut a banana tree and pound the trunk and leaves of the plant on a rock. Then we would mix the leaves with water and rice husks, and feed it to the pigs.

We never bought food from the market. We would go hunting or fishing and come home and cook what we caught. We would also collect wild plants, like wild bamboo shoots, vegetables, and fruits that grew all around us.

My grandmother was very smart. She never bought anything to use in the house; instead, she made everything herself, like mats from bamboo and pineapple plants, and she taught me to make everything myself too. She would make different sizes of containers out of bamboo so we could use them to collect sticks, vegetables, etc. Our house was built with wood but for the roof we used leaves from different trees. We made it all by hand.

We also made our own clothes. As there were no shops that sold clothes, everyone made their own clothes. My grandparents would travel to the town of Tavoy to buy cloth.

When I was young, I sold betel nut in the village to make extra money—not the betel leaves, just the raw betel nut that people would chew and spit out. We had betel trees, but my parents and grandparents didn't chew the nut, so we had spare nuts to sell.

Et Et was near the ocean, which we could reach by walking two to three hours, but we usually went by canoe. At the beach, we would swim and fish; I liked swimming, so I watched other people and taught myself to swim. My friends and I collected small clams and cooked them with a sour vegetable; sometimes we searched for big crabs. I used to love seafood, but now not as much because I know it's not good for my health.

I remember as a child that my life was very routine and every day I did the same daily chores. In the rainy season we would go to the farm and grow rice and in the hot season we made materials for the house.

At Christmas all the villagers would gather together in the church to celebrate and serve traditional Karen food like sticky rice. Sometimes we put it in leaves and boiled it in a pot; sometimes we fried the rice. The whole village ate together and gave presents, like books and pens, to the schoolchildren.

My village was a two-hour walk from a Burman Buddhist village called Kyauk Longyi. We used to be very friendly with the Burmans who had a shop and sold food. We didn't play too often with the Burman kids because it was too far away. There weren't many differences between the two villages except that they were Buddhist and we were Christian, and the languages we spoke were different. The relationship was quite good. I spoke Burmese, but I didn't understand Buddhism.

Before the Japanese invaded, my childhood was relaxed. At that time Burma was a British colony, but I never met any British people. We liked it when the British ruled Burma because it was peaceful time for us.

We had a village head and a few rules. If there was something important to announce, the head of the village would call a meeting and inform the villagers. There were never any problems in the village, but we had no medication or healthcare. If someone got sick, we used traditional medicine that the older people knew about. Some students studied in the town of Tavoy. When the Japanese invaded Burma in 1942, all the schools closed, and the students hurried back to their villages to warn everyone that the Japanese were coming. The Japanese planes began dropping bombs, so the villagers ran into the jungle.

Everyone from Et Et village ran to the foothills in Tavoy district. We all stayed in the jungle throughout the occupation. The Japanese weren't in the village, but people were afraid they would come or that they would bomb the village. We were also afraid that the Japanese would take us as porters.

I was ten years old and living with my grandparents when we ran from the Japanese. My parents were in a different village with my brother Htoo Htoo so they ran with the villagers in that area and went to a different place. I don't remember ever seeing my parents while we were in the jungle.

The children had to stay in the jungle, but the adults sometimes went back to Et Et to get supplies. They would check how everything was going and then come back to the jungle.

We didn't go to school; instead we helped cultivate food. We did slash and burn farming, felled trees, grew rice, and cleaned between the rows in the paddy fields. We cleared weeds every day until harvest. With the Japanese came insects that destroyed the crops. So, we had to go around and dig up *klee te* roots and eat it instead of rice. We worked very hard, but luckily my friends were there with me.

When we ran from the Japanese, we only had the clothes we were wearing, so almost everybody got body lice because we all had to wear the same clothes all the time. The body lice were very itchy and seventy years on I still have the scars from scratching. The lice were as big as a grain of rice and went under the skin. When the Japanese retreated, all the body lice retreated with them.

After a long time, our clothes decayed and fell apart. Some young girls, ashamed that they had no clothes to wear, thought about their lives and decided that they were not worth living. No one could really help them, as the girls were too shy to approach anyone with no clothes on. So they hanged themselves out of shame and sadness. Some Burmese ladies wore gunny (rice) bags. After one year, my clothes decayed and I too wore gunny bags for the next two years until the British came back.

I was not scared. We were young and innocent and didn't know how to be afraid. People didn't scare us. I was happy in the jungle.

In 1945 my grandmother died from diarrhea as there was no medical care during the Japanese occupation. I was with her when she was sick, and with her when she passed away. When she died, I cried and thought about her all the time. I was miserable and lonely and felt like I had lost part of myself. Sometimes I felt she was still alive and would walk through the door the way she usually did, even though I knew she was dead.

I never knew how my grandfather and the rest of my family felt about my grandmother's passing. In Karen culture, when people die, only older people talk to each other about what happened. They come together, grieve, and share their sorrow together. They help each other but they don't talk to their children about it.

Not long after my grandmother died, the Japanese left Burma. I remained with my grandfather, my aunt, and my aunt's husband and baby; then I returned to school. After my grandmother died, nothing changed, but I felt I was missing something in my life.

I lived away from my parents so my grandfather was more like my father and my grandmother more like my mother, who was always close to my heart. My grandmother taught me to sing songs, and when she tried to make my little cousin fall sleep in a hammock, she would ask me to sit with her to sing to the baby. We would sing together songs about heaven and happy songs about God: "When we arrive in heaven everything will be so peaceful and nice," and Pawpre would fall asleep listening to them.

BURMAN HARASSMENT

At this time the villagers had no sense of politics, so the Burmans often bullied them. The Burmans wanted to divide up the Karen villages so they looked to find fault with them and often blamed villagers for crimes in the area.

Soon after the Japanese left, one of the nearby Burman villages had a problem with robberies, and the villagers said that the burglar was a Karen. They accused my father of having a gun and instructing Karen villagers to rob the Burman village. The Burman villagers also accused my father of being close friends with the Japanese during the occupation. My father didn't have a gun, he wasn't a burglar, and he wasn't friends with the Japanese, but the villagers lied so that he would be arrested.

The Burmese military arrested my father together with one of my mother's cousins and, without a trial, they were taken to the Insein jail. We knew where they would be taken but we couldn't stop them.

When my father was arrested, my mother was pregnant with Ru Ru, so she found life difficult. She was very sad. I wasn't at home when he was arrested as I was staying with my grandfather. I would visit my mother whenever I had free time; usually I went twice a week. I did everything in the house: the cooking, cleaning, and washing. We hired someone to work in the paddy fields and paid them with the rice we harvested. We also raised chickens, ducks, and pigs and had fruit trees. At times we sold the fruit to buy clothing and other items. Overall, we had enough food to eat.

We were worried about my father being in jail, but we couldn't help him. My family wasn't able to go and visit him because the jail was so far away. And it wasn't possible to write either so we could not communicate with him.

My mother had her mother-in-law and my father's sister with her for support. When things go wrong, the family members support each other in the Karen tradition of mutual aid. This is important and normal for us. For example, during harvest time in my village everyone would come together and help each other to bring in the harvest.

One day I heard through the village elders that Burma would soon become independent of Britain. Every morning the village rang a bamboo bell and early in the morning of January 4, 1948, the day Burma won independence, every household in the village rang their bell at the same time. This was to inform everyone that Burma had gained independence.

I was too young to understand the consequences of independence. The villagers didn't know what independence meant or how it would affect them. They weren't very political.

However, not long after Burma's independence, the Karen Revolution started—on January 31, 1949, precisely. I didn't know about the revolution or the Battle of Insein as our village was quite isolated and we didn't have radio, television, or any form of communication with the world outside our little village.

The Burmese army thought our villagers were members of the Karen Revolution, so they attacked us and burned our village to the ground. We had nothing left and had had to run for our lives to the jungle. They burned down many Karen villages in our area. Once again, I was living with my grandfather when we had to flee, and my mother and siblings ran to a different place. We didn't know who went where.

One of my youngest aunts, my father's sister, was heavily pregnant at the time and could not run, so the Burmese soldiers shot and killed her. They shot a lot of people. One of my mother's cousins was fishing that day and the Burmese shot her dead when she ran. When I heard about their deaths, I was extremely frightened and scared. People were angry and cried; so did I.

I think the Burmese army launched widespread attacks on the Karen people because of the Battle in Insein, which I found out about only after I married my husband. After the Battle of Insein, the Karen soldiers fought the Burmese army. The Burmese army was staying with the Burman villagers in the area. So the Karen soldiers attacked and burned the Burman villages, after which the Burmans ran away and the army retreated.

Only when the Karen soldiers recaptured the village were we able to return. The soldiers stayed in the area to protect us and we loved the Karen soldiers because they helped us.

I, like all the villagers, was really happy to return to the village, even if we had to rebuild the houses with bamboo. But when we first returned we had no food as all the farms were burnt. However, Kyauk Longyi, where the Burmans had lived, had lots of stored rice and other food. When the KNLA occupied Kyauk Longyi, we went there to get rice and eggs since the Burman soldiers had all left.

After this we moved to a new village called Klaw Khwa, a day's walk from Et Et. My grandmother's cousin lived there, so we went to stay with her. Our villagers went to different places and I didn't know where everyone went.

I had finished seventh standard, the end of middle school, in 1948; afterwards I had to work to help other people and to get food. I was upset and depressed because I had moved to another village that I did not know. So I went to live with my mother, Htoo Htoo, and Ru Ru. My grandfather stayed with my youngest aunt in yet a different village. Our family was separated because there wasn't enough space for the family in one place. I felt lonely and missed them.

One day in 1952, after seven years in jail, my father came back to the village by himself. When my father came back the whole family was happy and we all stayed together. My father was older but he was still the same man. He took responsibility for all the farm work and bought more buffalo. He also helped my mother.

When I finally saw my father, it was really hard to call him "Dad" because we didn't live together. He had been away from us without any communication, first for one year during the occupation, and later for seven years. So, it was hard to say the word "Dad." As I grew up, I learned how to say "Dad." I practiced saying the word. It was difficult.

After my father came back my brother Ten Boy was born. There was a big age gap between him and me, the eldest. I was nineteen or twenty, the age when Karen women are usually married. My first boyfriend was my cousin, when I was sixteen or seventeen years old. My parents didn't want us to get married because we were related. So my parents decided to separate us. They sent my cousin to a Bible school, and me to another Bible school in Tavoy. We never saw each other again.

BIBLE SCHOOL
AND MISSIONARY WORK

In 1952 I went to Bible school in Tavoy for three years. I wasn't scared to leave my village as I went with some of my friends. To get to the school we traveled by boat to Tavoy, then by car from Tavoy to the school, which was on the edge of town. It was built on the corner of a big farm, and they had a girls' dormitory close to the school. The boys' dormitory was far from the school. The boys' and girls' dormitories were separate, but we had classes and meals together.

There were about fifty students at the school; they were Sgaw Karen, Pwo Karen and Mon. I was friends with everyone. I liked Bible school because we learned about God and the Bible. There I studied to be a teacher. The fees were quite high; I have no idea how much my parents paid.

After independence, the first Burmese government gave permission for the Bible schools to stay open. The Burmese army never attacked the Bible schools and the Burmese soldiers and the KNLA never interfered at the school. It was a peaceful time. After so much violence and the struggle to survive in the village, we were happy every day as students.

At Bible school, they taught three languages in different groups: Pwo Karen, Mon, and Sgaw Karen. They also call Pwo Karen "Mon Karen" because some of that language sounds like Mon and some is Burmanized. The Bible was available in all these languages. I joined with more groups so that I could learn more languages. I already knew the Sgaw and Pwo Karen languages, but I wanted to learn new languages. I chose the more challenging route because there are a lot of missionaries in the Karen community, but there are few Mon missionaries, so

I wanted to go there. Mon people are mainly Buddhist; I never studied Buddhism or any other religions, but I learned about them by myself through reading about other religions.

School went from 9 a.m. to 12 p.m. Then we had lunch and finished the day at 3 p.m. After school, we had to do homework. I was taught the whole Bible. We started with Genesis and studied through to Matthew. The teacher also taught us Proverbs, about the disciples, and the history of Paul and how the church started. Bible school was exciting. We would go on school camps and to other villages for missionary work.

We didn't have to memorize the Bible; we just had to understand it. The teachers, Baptist ministers, would give a lecture, and if we had a question, we would ask it. But we didn't discuss ideas like we do now in Bible study. Most of the teachers were men, but some women from Insein Bible School came to visit and give lectures.

In December we would have a Christmas pageant. We would tell the audience about God. We performed concerts where we sang Bible songs and told different stories. We sang many different Christmas songs. We went into the jungle, to Karen villages, to present our concerts.

Karen people like to be in the jungle because a long time ago they lived among other people who would fight and do bad things. Our people didn't want to live with the Mons or Burmans. They didn't want to fight so they went to live in the jungle where it was quiet and peaceful. No one else wanted to live in the jungle.

Because I was away from home at Bible school, there was no time to quarrel with my family when I came home. Every time we saw each other we were very happy.

Before Bible school, I didn't truly know about God, Jesus, and the Bible, but after studying at the school I changed. My faith had changed me. Before we were not very worldly people; if we had to shout, we would shout. If we were angry, we would be angry. Through learning the Scriptures, I understood I must be patient and share. I learned to control myself—as the Bible says—to do good things. My previous life was totally different; I didn't know how to control myself. If I felt angry, I would use curse words. But after studying the Bible I learned self-control. I learned how to do God's will. I learned a lot about myself and I changed.

We learned that no matter what happened with the Burmans or Karens, we had to give our problems to the Lord to worry about. In that way we could keep our minds clear, with no more hatred toward anyone. We learned to forgive. The Bible also says you must not take revenge. It is the Lord's problem to deal with.

If I hadn't studied at Bible school, I would have divorced my husband a long time ago because he used to like to drink all the time when he was younger. Every day when he would get drunk, I used to watch him. I remember trying to pray for him as he drank. The tears rolled down my face. Ralph would just say to me,

"It's raining today. The whole day it's raining." He didn't understand because he was drunk, so he just made a joke. But at Bible school I learned patience and self-control. The Bible said we couldn't be separated until God separated us at death.

I have doubted my faith in the past. When the children were sick, I would pray for them. I would get angry with God and question whether or not he was listening to me. After the children got better, I would feel better and stop questioning.

After Bible school, in 1955, I went to Thailand where Karen people also live, to do work for one year as a missionary in Ba Rain village near Kanchanburi. While I was a missionary, I taught the Thai Karen children at the local school.

I went to Ba Rain village because at the time only one household in the village was Christian. The household knew the principal of the Bible school, so they requested two missionaries to come and teach at the school. I was selected to go with a friend called Baw Baw.

The lessons were all in Karen, not in Thai. I lived with the head of the village. He wasn't Christian but rather animist. We taught the children to read and after they learned to read Karen, they read the Bible and became Christian. More missionaries came after us and the whole village became Christian.

Karens in Thailand have a different accent but their lifestyles are the same as ours in Burma. They live in the hills and in the remote areas. So, for me it was the same as being on the Burmese side of the border. It was an adventure for me.

When we were living in Thailand, two Thai villagers fell in love with Baw Baw and me. They lived in a different village but would come to visit a Thai villager called Maw Bu in our village. We didn't speak Thai and they didn't speak Karen, so Maw Bu would interpret for us. They wrote us letters professing their love for us, but Maw Bu never gave the letters to us. Instead he wrote back a letter pretending to be us and telling them we liked them too. Maw Bu did this because our suitors would bring him food, whiskey, and presents. The Thai villagers told us that they looked at the letter that we (supposedly) wrote and concluded that we were in love with them.

They came to visit us to ask us to wash their clothes, but we were not home. This was a tradition in many Asian cultures: that the girlfriends or wives would wash the clothes of their men. Men didn't do domestic chores in these cultures; women did everything. When we came back, the owner of the house where we were living told us what had happened.

The two Thai villagers planned to run away with us to get married. At that time there were lots of robberies and they told the other villagers we were spies or robbers. They went to the head of the village and told him the story. They asked him to bring his elephant. They told Baw Baw and me that they were taking us by elephant to Ta Ka Naw village because we were spies, but when we arrived they had actually taken us to Plaw Ka Say village. Two of the Karen villagers, including the village chief, had come with us because they were suspicious of the two Thai men. They wanted to look after me and Baw Baw. Plaw Ka Say was a Thai village of Mons and Karens. We stayed at a Mon house, all five of us: two Karen men, us, and the elephant handler. The Thai men told us to stay there and they stayed in a different house.

The next night, the two Thai men came to see us. One of the Karen men asked, "Why do you want these two women to leave the village? For what purpose?" They explained to the Karen men that they had fallen in love with us and from the letter they saw, it looked like we loved them too. After that, the Karen men asked us if we loved them. "If you love them, we won't bother you. If you don't, we won't let them take you." We told them that we didn't love them and we didn't write the letter.

The two Karen men, Baw Baw, and I decided to go home that night. But the Mon household didn't want us to go at night because it would be too dangerous. The Thai men had lots of friends and the Mons were worried that someone would follow us. They said we should go in the morning, so we did.

The two Thai men followed us with guns. Halfway back to the village, they told the village chief to ask Baw Baw and me to get down from the elephant. But the Karen man had already told us that if the chief told us to get down, we shouldn't do so. So, we didn't get down from the elephant. If we had gotten down, they may have forced us to go with them. The elephant was male, had tusks that were very sharp, and was a bit wild. So, they didn't dare get close to the elephant. Then the Karen men said that the situation wouldn't end here and we would have to go back to Maw Bu to resolve the problem.

I was very scared that the Thai men would force us to go with them. Baw Baw was also scared. We held hands very tightly. We were also afraid the Karen and Thai men would shoot each other. We went back to our village where the chief resolved the problem with the Thai men and after one year, we returned to Burma and went to Mon State.

I went to teach in a Mon village, Pizanklo. I was the only Karen in Pizanklo. I felt happy because I was teaching people who didn't know and understand God. I would teach about the Bible as well as teaching the students to read and write in Mon. It was the same teaching the Mons as the Karens. I enjoyed teaching both.

They had a small school with about twenty children. I was the only teacher. My students were about ten or twelve years old. I liked being a teacher because I taught the children to grow up in a spiritual way. The Mons wanted me there because they wanted their children to be educated. The parents were illiterate so when I taught their children to read and write the parents were very happy.

As a missionary, I didn't receive any payment, though I was given money and food as offerings. Offerings were given to me for praying in someone's house. There was no regular pay, but it was enough to live on.

The villagers liked me, and they were friendly. They were all Buddhists. I lived with a Buddhist religious leader who was ordained; all his family had religious positions in the Buddhist faith. The father studied the *Sebah Thila*, the Buddhist scriptures, as did his wife and his daughter, but I had studied none. We would talk sometimes about faith and religion. I told the religious leader about Jesus coming to save our lives. He died for our sins, and that's why we were released from our sins. But Buddhists are different; if they give more, they will receive more. It didn't matter that I was Christian in a Buddhist village. No one became Christian while I was there, but some people did later.

Once, while I was living with the family, no one was home and I felt hungry. They had a Buddhist statue with an offering. I was hungry, so I ate the offering. Afterwards the family came home and laughed at me. They said, "The Christian girl eats twice a day, but the statue only eats once a day."

I taught the children how to sing and at Christmas I used to take them to other Christian villages to sing carols. They were very happy. Later on, when I was married, my husband would say, "Sing how you used to sing when you were single."

The children were quite innocent. They wanted to learn so they were easy to teach—and they weren't naughty. I was happy to teach because the children got an education. I combined literacy with scripture so that scripture went into their heads.

I once had to travel to Rangoon for a religious meeting in Ahlone, the Karen quarters outside Rangoon. After we attended the meetings and before coming back, we saw the Shwedagon Pagoda and some other places. When I saw Shwedagon I was very tired. I felt tired for the Buddhists who had to go and get water, take it to the top, and pour it on the idols.

After one year in Pizanklo, I was sent to a Buddhist Pwo Karen village in Paing Kyon (Ta Kreh) in Hpa An District. I stayed there teaching for another year before I moved to Pe Krew in the Hlaingbwe area in 1958. In the village there was a stream with people living on both sides. Christians were living on one side and Buddhists on the other side, but it was one village. My students were both Christian and Buddhist. I liked all the villagers. The Burmese army came only once while I was living in Hlaingbwe. They targeted a Karen forester who lived there with his family and burned his house.

I became a lay minister in Pe Krew because they had no pastor. I continued to preach after I was married. Sometimes people would ask me to preach at a special event like a birthday party and I would. I think people asked me because they knew I went to Bible school and because I was older. I still like preaching and I still do some.

I also taught Sunday school. I love teaching Sunday school because it's good to teach the children to know God's word. They will want to do good things. I want the next generation to have a better life and do good.

MARRIAGE

I first met my husband, Ralph Hodgson, when I was teaching in Pe Krew village in Hlaingbwe township. He was stationed with the KNLA there. He knew the couple that I was living with. Before I went to the house in the village, Ralph used to call the couple I lived with "Mum and Dad." Every time Ralph went to the village, he stayed with that couple. But when I was living there, he would go and stay at a different house. When he came to visit them, he met me.

When I first met him, I wasn't interested in him, but he kept writing many letters to me. In the first letter he said, "But you I saw, but you I admired, but you I adore." Although Ralph wrote many letters to me, I never wrote back. Then he sent me an empty letter and envelope so I could write to him. He started coming to visit the family and started to ask me questions face to face. He asked about the letters he sent and whether I received them or not. He said, "I wrote you many letters, so I want to get letters back from you." I also wanted letters back from him. We fell in love through letters. Later I wrote back to Ralph saying I had fallen in love with him. I wrote in the letter, "I hope that I can fulfill your needs."

There were other men who wrote letters to me, but they were not in my mind because I was concentrating on my work. I didn't bother with them. After I had fallen in love with my husband, some men still wrote to me through him and he brought those letters to me. The other suitors were either other villagers or other soldiers in the KNLA.

I had a three-year courtship with Ralph, but we never discussed marriage. When we met, we would be shy because we were not close friends. We didn't see each other very often. I saw him maybe three times per year, so maybe nine times altogether before we were married. We were never close to each other. As I was the leader of the church, I had to behave properly.

Soldiers didn't get paid, so when it came to personal affairs, the unit commander had to take responsibility because he had a fund for them. The KNLA had a meeting and asked whether, in the coming years, any of the men wanted to get married. Some of Ralph's friends said they would marry. Most of Ralph's friends knew that he had a girlfriend, so they tried to push him to stand up and say he was going to get married that year too.

The KNLA leaders organized the ceremony for Ralph and me, but I didn't know anything about it at the time. He had sent a letter to me through the KNU, but the man didn't deliver it. Instead, I went back to Hpa-An not knowing I was missing my own wedding! Ralph waited for me to come but when the time came, I hadn't arrived. The other couples married, but Ralph and I didn't.

The elders had a meeting and they talked about us. They discussed their points of view about whether we should get married and how it would be for us. I was present at the meeting and I heard them say at this meeting that out of all the youths that were single, he was the best natured and very patient. Because he courted me by writing and then I heard them talk about him like that, I knew marriage to him would be quite safe for me.

I wasn't worried that he would die in the war. Not only soldiers die but even children can die too, so that was separate from my thoughts.

In a traditional Karen hill tribe wedding, if two people are in love, they ask some elders to make the match. The parents from both sides must agree. Then they call *nats* (spirits), slaughter pigs, have a feast, and do a wrist-tying ceremony. When the groom goes to the bride, both are accompanied by their relatives and friends, who play drums, gongs, and large cymbals. The groom goes with his friends and relatives to the bride's house and the party stops outside the house. Then the bride and her friends and relatives come out carrying drums. They all make a lot of noise and follow the groom to a place where they have built a roof. This is where they will have the celebrations. Both sides sing and recite poetry. One side says something and the other side replies. Karen men don't usually wear a wedding ring; usually only the bride wears a wedding ring. The Christian Karens have Western-style Christian weddings, but with no alcohol.

We had to wait a few months to get married. I was ready to get married. I was twenty-eight and Ralph was thirty when we were married. I was older than most Karen women are when they marry.

The day before our wedding, January 31, 1961, was Resistance Day, the celebration of the day we started our revolt against the Burmese. On Resistance Day, there are always many visitors in the area, so we wouldn't know who's who. We decided to wait and have the wedding the next day.

I didn't know what to expect on my wedding day because we didn't organize anything. We had a Western-style Christian wedding. None of our family was there. I felt sorry that none of my relatives or my parents was there. But we were very far from our families. We just celebrated with our own friends and the village elders. The Burmese army was in Hlaingbwe, so we could not be married there because they could attack at any time. We were married in Pway Htaw Roe village in the foothills where it was safer.

After most Karen villagers are married, the bride stays with her parents and the groom comes to live with them. Nowadays it's different. Sometimes the bride goes to live with the groom's family.

Two or three days after we got married, Ralph went to the front line. During those first three days, I felt like I had a friend as well as a husband. Then, after he left, I felt very lonely and missed him. I looked out for him every day. Sometimes we could write letters.

When the soldiers came back to the village, I particularly missed him and watched for him to come back. I was never angry with him for leaving. I knew he had a responsibility, a duty, to the revolution. Soldiers don't have any choice when they have to go.

When I asked Ralph why he didn't stay with me, why he would go away, he asked me, "Weren't you a teacher before? If the teacher is not there, what will happen to the students? If I'm not there, what will happen to the soldiers?" I understood Ralph well. I knew before I got married what life would be like with a soldier. A soldier's life is not easy. You cannot always be together.

After Ralph and I were married, I stayed with a family of KNU officials in the hills. If I had stayed in Pe Krew, I would have been alone. News had spread that I married an officer, so it was too dangerous. A Burmese government soldier could come at any time from Hlaingbwe and attack me.

The KNU helped us so I had enough food. They provided supplies for the house where I stayed, including rice, chilies, and fish paste. During the day I grew vegetables and gardened. I found fish, little crabs, and prawns in the streams. When I stayed with that family, I was like a family member, so I had to help cook and clean like a family member.

Six months after he left, Ralph came home. He only stayed for one week. After that, he was sometimes away for three months, eight months, or even a year. I had no idea where he was because he was mobile. Sometimes I saw a couple walking by and I wanted to walk like them. They could walk together but I had to walk alone.

I stayed with the KNU family for quite a long time. Then I went to stay back in Pe Krew because my marriage was old news.

My brothers got married but I never went to either of their weddings. When Ru Ru's wife was pregnant, they were attending a football match. The Burmese army began shelling the village. Everyone ran away from the shelling. Ru Ru and his wife took cover when a shell exploded near them. It killed Ru Ru, but his wife and the baby survived.

Htoo Htoo died of mouth cancer when he was older. When my brothers died, I was away, and I didn't see them or their families. Because I married Ralph, I was separated from my family with the Burmese army in between. I dared not cross the Burmese army's territory to see my family. My father came once to visit in about 1968 and he met my husband.

I was around sixty years old when my father died. He was about eighty years old then. My mother was about seventy years old when she died. When my mother died, I was with my husband, so I don't know exactly when she died.

When Ralph was back, I felt more encouraged because he was always able to ask for things for me. When he was there, and I needed something, he would ask the neighbor to come and help me. When I needed firewood, Ralph organized firewood for the whole rainy season so I didn't need to look for it.

I was scared that one day I would be told he had been killed. Every day I prayed for him. When I heard that he had to go to the front line, I would pray for him. I was scared whenever I heard there was gunfire or fighting. I would ask all the time, "Is he all right? Has something happened to him?" It became normal. I was not the only one feeling this. Everyone who marries a soldier knows this situation and this feeling.

CHILDREN

After two years of marriage, in 1963, I had my first son, Dey Law. Before I gave birth, Ralph organized a place for me to go and live in a village with a midwife. They built a house for me and I lived alone. The night I gave birth to Dey Law, the frogs were croaking really loudly, so the house owner decided to call him "frog croak." Karen people often do this. Sometimes when a VIP comes, they name the child after them. There are lots of "Ralphs" in Kawthoolei named after my husband.

Two weeks after I gave birth, Ralph came and visited Dey Law and me. I felt happy we were all together, but he didn't know how to behave because he was new to being a father. He was drinking a lot at that time and after a few days he had to go back to the front line.

I was very happy with Dey Law. I loved playing with him. When he was a few months old he became sick with malaria. I prayed to God, "If you want him to be with you, call him back." If God wanted him, he should take him. He passed away.

I was living alone and was basically a single mother with no family around. With my first child, I didn't know how to look after him. I didn't have any experience. When he had a fever, I didn't know what to do, and there were no hospitals. There was no one to ask what to do. It was really hard. With the older children, I had experience and I prepared a first aid kit. I learned traditional medicine, so I knew what to do. Everyone got malaria; no one escaped. Sometimes the children died.

I didn't write a letter to Ralph to tell him Dey Law had died because there was no one to take it to him. At the time, he had a meeting in Papun. It was a long distance away. I asked one of the staff members from the signals department to send a message to him that his son had died.

Ralph never really spent time with Dey Law and they didn't have a relationship, so he always thought of our second son, Ler Paw, as his first child. But for me, I had two months with Dey Law. Only I had a relationship with him.

We never spoke about Dey Law's death. It was really sad for both of us. We didn't talk about it because it was so sad. I wanted to talk about it but I knew even if I spoke to Ralph, he couldn't do anything about it.

After Dey Law died, I felt miserable. I cried every day. When I heard the pig scream, it sounded like a baby crying. I would think of Dey Law and how I used to look after him and carry him when he cried. Sometimes I saw other children run by and I'd get up and run after them, but it was not my son. I just kept doing housework. One of the ladies came and stayed with me to help.

A year later I fell pregnant again. When I was eight months pregnant the Burmese army attacked Ler Dah, where I was living. When I saw them, I ran. Everyone ran in different directions. With my big tummy I swam across a small river to the other side where there were fields. I crossed the rice fields until I reached the big Paw Klo River. I got to the river and saw a boat and asked the boat driver to take me across the river. He said, "No, you can go and stay with the Karen soldiers over there." I said I was scared to stay with the Karen soldiers in case they had to fight. So he took me to the other side of the river.

Then there was a small hill. I could hear the machine gun bullets going "Phwa! Phwa!" behind me. I couldn't see anyone else because everyone ran in different directions. I was really scared. I was told that if there was shooting, I needed to lie down and pretend to be dead. But when I heard the bullets, I just ran. Only when the bullets stopped could I relax.

I went to the other side and climbed up the hill. I was scared that with my pregnant stomach they might kill me. So, I ran very fast. I looked and I could see the rice fields. I climbed into the water and submerged my body with just my mouth above the water, so I could breathe. It was winter, so the water was very cold. I was terrified that the Burmese army might see me and kill me.

After a little over half an hour I looked around. At first, I didn't see anyone but when the fighting finished I stood up and saw the other villagers. The Burmese soldiers had gone.

I went and spoke to nearby villagers. While we talked, Karen soldiers came back from the fighting and we learned that one of the Karen officers, Bo San Kyi, had died in the battle.

This was a time of guerrilla warfare. The Burmese army usually entered like guerrillas. They would come into the village quietly. No one knew when they came. The KNLA soldiers had come to the village looking for food. The Burmese army came and captured one of the KNLA soldiers. They questioned him and asked where his leader lived. He told them that he lived close to the mountains and showed them where the other KNLA soldiers were.

As soon as I see danger, I run. I had to run from the Japanese soldiers and then the Burmese army. I didn't go back to my house because I was so scared. My husband was away and hadn't been home for three months. With the aid of a friend, I went to stay with someone in Hlaing Da. He was Buddhist and became uncomfortable about me, a Christian woman, giving birth in his house. One day he got drunk and told me he didn't want me to give birth there because my husband was important and he was afraid he could get into trouble.

My friend then took me to a river where they had a small little hut near the water for me. But I had no one to look after me there. I looked out of the hut and saw a Burmese soldier walking around, so I left the little hut. I went to my friend again and she found me a midwife and a place to stay with a widow and her children and grandchildren.

Because of the pregnancy I smelled a lot and my hosts asked me to leave. They again looked for another place for me. I moved to another house where a midwife lived, and there I gave birth to my second son, Ler Paw, on March 5, 1965.

Ralph had to go to another brigade that was far away. When Ler Paw was six or seven months old, Ralph came back. By that time, Ler Paw knew how to crawl.

The villagers had built a new hut for me in Ler Dah village in the Kaw Ka Reik area. I had a little village girl called Ma Yin Kwet stay with me to help me with housework.

Karens have a custom there. Those who are in the revolution are not free to stay with their families, so if the wives face any hardships, the villagers are responsible for helping them. They know the husband is not free, so the people have the responsibility to help her.

After Ler Paw was born I couldn't produce milk for him, so I boiled rice and made it into a paste to give him. At nighttime I would give him rice porridge. Sometimes I gave him sugar cane juice. I went all over the village to other women who had young children and had them feed him. The women would feed him on their way to catch fish and again on their way home. One woman after another helped me. I was very skinny at the time. I didn't have enough nutrients in my body to produce milk. As he grew up he could eat more rice and chicken, or fish soup mixed with rice. No one told me what to do to raise my children. I just came up with the ideas.

When Ler Paw was small, we were both captured. The Burmese army was holding a meeting and they didn't want the KNLA to attack. They devised a strategy to capture one of the officers' wives so the KNLA wouldn't attack. I was afraid. I knew they wouldn't kill me, but I thought they might put me in prison. I was scared about sexual assault because they were all men and I was the only woman. They were the enemy, they weren't friends, and I had no idea what they would do.

I had heard that the Burmese officer in charge was notorious: that he was very harsh and that he would lock people up far away. One day I was praying by the river. The officer went down to fish. He came up to me and said, "Sister, I couldn't get any fish for you. I only got one little prawn." The way he spoke was so gentle.

When they captured us, I told the officer in charge of the Burmese army that I wanted someone to accompany me because I was really scared something would happen to me. The leader told me not to worry and that if anything happened, I should go to him immediately. "If someone is violent towards you, come and see me." Not all the Burmese military officers were like that. He told me that if something happened to Ler Paw, I should come and tell him, and he would get a medic to look after him. There were medics where they took me. Saw Ler Paw had a skin rash, and the Burmese medic helped him.

One day I heard the soldiers singing Christian hymns and worshiping. They were Chin, and Christians too![1] There were very few Christians in the Burmese army, so I felt that God was looking after me. I knew that if they were Christian, they wouldn't be barbarous or rough with me. I felt reassured.

At the time, Ler Paw could walk but he didn't know what was going on. He was playing with the children of the army. He didn't know they were the enemy. The Burmese leader joked, "The KNLA officer's son isn't afraid of anything."

An officer told me they would take me to the Moulmein jail. One of the Burmese military leaders told me not to worry. They would have a meeting and he would speak on my behalf, saying I should be released because only the men were fighting, not the women. When the meeting happened, the leader spoke on my behalf. In their rules and regulations, they are not allowed to release a wife unless five villagers say she should be released. The officer organized five villagers to come to the meeting and say I should be freed.

After the meeting, the officer came to see me and asked if I wanted to go home, and I said yes. After the meeting, I was released. The officer told the five villagers, "When you take her, make sure you look after her because she has a baby." I don't think he did this just because I had a baby. It was just his personality; he was a good man.

When I was released, the soldiers called after me and said, "Sister, sister, we're Christian too." I think they looked after us because they were Chins and

---

1. The Chin are one of the ethnic nationalities in Burma. The Chin State on the India frontier is one of the poorest territories in the country, and in the past young Chin men have joined the Burmese army for a paid job. Like other minorities, they have rarely achieved high rank.

they were also Christians. I think the incident happened that way because of God. I prayed, and he looked after me.

When I was captured, I only had one longyi. The officer gave some money to the village leader's wife and asked her to buy me a new one. The other villagers came and helped me and gave me some clothes. The villagers heard that the Burmese army had captured a woman but she only had one longyi. When I came home, another lady in the village joked, "If I had known that they would be so generous like that, I would have wanted to get captured too"—to get a new longyi!

After my capture, the Burmese army knew where I lived so I moved to another village called Pi Ta Ka. I had to move to another place where the Burmese army didn't know where I was.

My third son, Ler Gay (James), was born there in September 1968. The midwife helped me give birth without any problems. I still couldn't produce milk, but I could buy milk powder to feed him.

Pi Ta Ka was far away from any Burman villages and close to the mountains. Other wives of KNLA military lived there. They could come and go. I had friends there. I asked someone to come and live with me. Naw Kaser, one of the villagers in Pi Ta Ka, came and lived with me to help me.

I grew my own vegetables, all different types. Every day I would look after the children, wash clothes, and look for food like wild vegetables. I would go fishing with a net in the river. I would catch small fish and prawns. I would cook them for us to eat.

The most fun for me was feeding the animals. I would feed the chickens, pigs, ducks, goats, and turkeys once every day. This was the part of my day when I would relax. All day I was busy trying to find food to survive, so this was my favorite time, when I could watch the animals grow. The goat had a baby and the pig had ten piglets. The babies were really cute. We had a fence to keep animals out of the vegetable area. I had to make the fence myself. I had to stand on my own two feet.

I also had a small banana plantation. I had to get up early in the morning before dawn to pick the banana tree leaves for the roof of the house. At that time of day, the dew fell on the leaves and the leaves were soft. When the sun came up, it would make them go hard and we could not put them in the basket. We picked them on the slope of the hill by the river. We came home, ate, then used bamboo to make the roof. Everybody did the same thing. So, at dawn, everybody went to pick the leaves and I had to catch up to them. It was very social, and we all talked while we walked.

There was a church in the center of the village. It was big enough for all the villagers, about seventy to eighty people. I felt happy when I went to church. I could thank God and be grateful for everything: for looking after me, for food every day, for our lives, and for our health.

In 1971 it was not safe in the village, so we moved to Kler Thay Lu village at the Thai-Burma border, about twenty kilometers from where Ralph was living in Manerplaw. I was pregnant with my fourth child. While I was pregnant I caught pneumonia. There were no doctors or medication there, so it got worse and worse. By the time I got to a hospital it was almost hopeless. The doctor told me that I would have to stay in the hospital for about a year. At one stage, my lungs were full of water and pus and the doctor said I was going to have to take an injection every day for about ten days. I had to leave my small children with somebody else. I prayed to God and said, "If you are there, intervene and let me stay in the hospital for only ten days." After ten days, they told me I could be discharged and that I would not die of this disease. If I had been faithless, I think I would have died.

I had to go over a mountain to go back to where I was living, but I was too unwell. Ralph only came to visit me in the hospital once. Ralph built a hut for me in a closer village, on the Burmese side of the border, and they brought the children to me.

On November 15, 1971, when I was almost due to give birth, I was on the Moei River bank near Mae Ta Waw when the Burmese army attacked and we all had to run again. This time I had three children with me: Ler Paw and Ler Gay, who were very small, and their cousin.

We fled to the Thai side of the border and squatted in one of the slash-and-burn huts. I had malaria and all night long I was burning up. A lady happened to come by looking for fish. I told her that I thought I was going to give birth tonight and I didn't have anyone to help me. I asked her if she knew how to give birth to a baby, and she replied no. I asked to just stay with me for the night and we could do what I had done during my previous childbirth experiences. I asked her to get some water from the stream.

When I went into labor, I massaged my belly and the baby came out feet first. She was very small. There was nothing to cut the umbilical cord with. There was a knife, but it was very dirty. So, I put water on some hot coals and put it on the umbilical cord to sterilize it. I didn't have any thread to tie the umbilical cord, but the lady had a Shan bag with tassels. She took some tassels from the bag and used it to tie the umbilical cord.

By the morning the lady was gone. My baby, a girl, was fine. The other children had been running around throughout the labor before going to sleep. The cousin went to pick some wild vegetables and cooked me some curry. She also washed my clothes for me. We all stayed in the hut for one week. At night I was scared because I could hear tigers roaring in the jungle. The hut was quite isolated. Ralph came home about a month after Mina was born and stayed for about a week.

We stayed in Me Twe village for one year after she was born. We then moved to where the Karen engineers were in Mae Tan, south of Mae Sot. When we would get news of a Burmese army offensive, we crossed the Moei River and stayed in an old hut in Thailand.

We moved around a lot when the children were small. If we moved temporarily, if the situation was not good in the area, people would help us move. We would go to another village and just take our most important possessions. We didn't take our livestock or crops. We just took clothes, food, and the barest essentials. We would come back when the situation improved.

I liked having a girl. It was a full family with boys and a girl. When Mina was a small girl, she had dark skin, so we called her Kawlamu in Karen, meaning Indian girl. But she didn't like the name. When she was three or four years old, one of her friends called her Amina, in an Indian language. She didn't know what it meant but she came home and said, "I want to be called Mina. Don't call me Kawlamu anymore; call me Mina." When she came to Australia she changed her name to Flavia because she liked the name, but we still call her Mina.

Ler Paw is named after a precious stone that is a pink color. I named him that because a good stone can become a good man. Also, a good stone is a good foundation. It is hard and strong. I wanted him to grow up firm and strong. Ler Gay is also the name of a good stone: like a diamond. I wanted them to grow up on a solid foundation. That is what every mother wants. I didn't want them to join the KNLA. I wanted them to study, be educated, and live with their parents. But it wasn't my decision to say what they should do. If they wanted to serve the revolution, it was up to them.

Paw Ney Tha (Judith) was born at Kler Thay Lu on the Thai-Burma border in 1973 with a doctor there. For the first time, Ralph was home too.

I had many friends in Kler Thay Lu village and some were soldiers' wives. It was difficult to have small children with my husband always away. I had to look after my children the way a widow looked after her children, without a husband. We would talk about how hard it was with our husbands away. All the soldiers' wives struggled on their own. We had no time to help others. We were all busy with the same lifestyle. Every day I would ask God to help me, to give me strength to get through.

When my husband came home, sometimes my children thought he was a visitor because they did not recognize him. Only when they got a little bigger could they remember that he was their father. When they asked about their father, I told them he was an army officer. I said that if he came home there would be no one to look after the soldiers there, so he could only come back once in a while and not for long because he has to go back and look after the soldiers. They missed Ralph when he went away for a short time, but when he was away for a long time, they would forget about him. They weren't naughty and they helped me.

When my children were small, they would play with each other and sometimes they would fight. My children would play with large round seeds, maybe five centimeters (about two inches) in diameter. They would roll them to hit something. The game was called *Maw ke tha*. The seeds were like beans. The children used to flick them or roll them, similar to bowls or marbles. There were no toys, so they had to make their own.

When the children needed medical help, I took them to the clinic at Palu customs gate in Karen State. The first time I went to the Palu clinic, they didn't have the medicine or equipment we needed so they sent us across the border to Mae Sot in Thailand. We stayed there for two days. I didn't speak Thai, but I had a friend there, Ma Nu, who helped me.

When Ler Gay was about eleven years old he developed kidney problems. He became very bloated. People kept telling me, "This boy won't live." People kept saying to find bamboo and then boil it and give the water to him. I didn't question them because it was the only information I had. I went and boiled it for him and he felt better each time. They told me his kidney had been destroyed—it was already gone. When I took him to the hospital in Kler Thay Lu, they didn't know what to do with him. The doctors told me that even in England that couldn't cure a disease like this in this condition. The doctor told me not to give him salt; he had too much salt. We moved him to Palu and we managed to send him to the hospital in Thailand where they gave him the medicine he needed.

It was very common to go to Thailand. I would often go to the KNU bases at Palu and Wangkha gates when Ralph was there. We would visit him and then go across to Thailand. We used KNU papers to cross the border. The KNU would write a permission letter to get people across.

I had a Burmese identity card before I was married. After I was married I couldn't use it anymore because I married a KNLA soldier, a rebel in the eyes of the Burmese authorities. So, when I married, I lost my Burmese identity. I don't feel "Burmese" so I wasn't sad to give this up. When I married Ralph, I didn't care about the identity card and what I was giving up. I only cared about my children and the future. It was the right decision.

In 1983 I moved to Htoo Wah Lu on the Thai side of the border near the KNU headquarters at Manerplaw, where Ralph was stationed. I could then go to visit Ralph where he was working about twice a year. I would call first to see if he was there. I wouldn't go if he was at the front line because I didn't want to risk going there. When he wasn't fighting, I would go to visit him because I missed him. I would take the children because he wanted to see them. We would go for three or four days. It was short because he would have to go back to the front line. We were always separated, and he was always going away, so it was very normal for me.

Our house in Htoo Wah Lu was on stilts, with a ladder. The animals were underneath or beside the house. The house was bigger than our house in Perth today. You could plant vegetables all the way back. I had catfish as well. Whenever I came home I would go straight to the stream to watch them and relax. KNU soldiers and villagers built my house. I could choose the location, but I had to organize the building and materials. There was one road, with houses on both sides and the stream and mountains nearby.

Sometimes Ralph would come to Htoo Wah Lu once a week, sometimes once a month. When he came to visit more often, I felt more secure. When he came back or was in Manerplaw, I didn't have to worry about his safety. When he was away, and I heard there was a bombing or deaths, I would worry. But I could also see him when I was in Manerplaw.

My youngest child, Paw Nay Thah, was born healthy. But at ten years of age, something happened to her. She got a fever; I was scared and called a medic. He injected her with a medicine called Novalgin in her bottom, which was commonly used for malaria. After that she couldn't move her leg. I was really upset because if she couldn't walk that would cause lots of problems for the whole family. We would need to look after and watch her all the time. Ler Paw was about eighteen and studying in Palu. Ler Gay and Mina had to help with Paw Nay Thah. It was very difficult. I trained her to do exercises to learn how to walk again and that's why she can walk now. It took her almost a year to relearn how to walk.

At the time that my brother Htoo Htoo died of mouth cancer, his wife had already died of cancer before him. So their children, La Ku and her sister Ta Kaw Paw, came to live with us. They were young, about ten, when he died.

It was a very busy time. I needed to find food for myself and for all my children. Looking after the family was very difficult. We raised domestic animals, so we had to find food for them as well as ourselves.

Mina and James went to study in Palu too. Education was really important for us. They would need good jobs for when they were grown up and had families: easier jobs, so they wouldn't have to work hard to survive like Ralph and I did.

Both Ralph and I were educated. This was rare for Karens. My children all went to high school. I didn't need to pay any money for their education because the KNU paid for their education. The KNU schools were also free. Everyone helped each other so we didn't need to pay for the things we needed. Nobody had money.

Health care was free. It was supported by donations from international NGOs (nongovernmental organizations). It wasn't good quality, but it was OK. We had hospitals in Htoo Wah Lu and Hpway Baw Lu. Médicins Sans Frontières came and helped. We had X-ray machines but no materials for operations. If someone needed an operation, they sent them to Thailand and paid the costs. When my husband had hepatitis, he went to Thailand. I went as far as Mae Sot with him, and he went on to Chiang Mai alone. I couldn't go because I didn't have any documents. He could only go because he was a patient and the Thai government turned a blind eye.

After Ler Paw finished high school, he joined the KNU's forestry department and lived in Mae La in the KNLA Seventh Brigade area. Ler Gay went to Thailand after high school. He learned more English and Thai. After finishing school, Mina studied English at Noe Boe school on the Thai border where they had foreign teachers. She then came to Australia on a refugee visa. First she worked, then she attended the Riverview International Church Bible School in Perth. She lived with her uncle Howard, who sponsored her.

Ler Paw married first, on May 23, 1994, in Htee Thay Kee, close to Manerplaw. I was at his wedding. I really like Ler Paw's wife. She's a mix of Sgaw and Pwo Karen. I first met her when I came and visited her in Mae La. I didn't know they were together. Later he came and saw me and told me that he had a girlfriend. I was happy when they got married.

Not long after Ler Paw was married, Ler Gay also got married to a Thai-Karen woman. They got married at the registry office in Chiang Mai, so I wasn't there.

After high school, Paw Nay Thah left Htoo Wah Lu to study English and Thai in Thailand. She met an '88 Generation Burmese student named Lwin Moe who was involved in the '88 protests and escaped to Manerplaw. He was a computer trainer. The students had an office in Chiang Mai as well. Paw Nay Thah participated in the computer training where they met. Later they got married in Bangkok.

After high school all my children went away. This was normal. I felt happy that they were going away for their education and to better their lives.

After Mina was born, the Burmese army didn't attack near me for a very long time. It felt peaceful and we were safe. I always knew that there was a war going on somewhere but it was far from where we were living. I was able to find some safety, even in such a long war.

15

THE KAREN WOMEN'S ORGANIZATION

The Karen Women's Organization (KWO) met on April 5, 1985, to reestablish and reorganize itself.[1] All the women who lived near Manerplaw were invited and I joined because I wanted to do something for the Karen women and for the future.

KWO membership was open to all Karen women eighteen years and older, from all religions. Girls under eighteen were could join the Karen Youth Organization (KYO), which had its own constitution and was also under the KNU.

At its first meeting the KWO held elections for leadership positions ranging from chairwoman, vice chairwoman, general secretary, treasurer, and auditor down to the organizers of the different departments such as health, education, welfare, and organization. There were some twenty members involved in our organization. As the KWO was under the KNU, some KWO departments like the education department reported to a parallel department of the KNU.

Usually the KNU president's wife was the KWO president, so Bo Mya's wife, Naw Lah Po, became the KWO president after the 1985 meeting. Naw Lah Po was younger than me by about fifteen or twenty years and I had met her while I lived in Htoo Wah Lu.

---

1. The Karen Women's Organization was first established in 1949 and is a community-based organization of Karen women working in development and relief in the refugee camps on the Thai-Burma border and with Internally Displaced Persons and women inside Burma. In March 2019, the current general secretary of the KWO, Naw K'Nyaw Paw, was awarded an "International Women of Courage" award by the US Secretary of State.

Ka Prey was elected vice chairwoman and treasurer, and Mwe Paw was elected general secretary. Paw Rae was elected joint secretary. I, along with Cho Thein, had the role of organizer in the Organization Department at our central office in Manerplaw.

We were all like sisters in the KWO, passionate about our work and enjoying what we did. My closest friends were Pee Thoo Lei, Naw Lah Po, Ku Paw, Shwe Paw, May Htoo, Myaing Po, and Ka Prey. These women were my KNU family before we began the KWO. I had known many of them for a long time as many lived in Htoo Wah Lu and our children were all friends.

Some people called Pee Thoo Lei, Naw Lah Po, and me "the ladies." We were a tight threesome of friends that had been teachers before were married. We were sometimes likened to a brand of sardines called Three Lady Sardines. We discussed everything and if we had a problem, we would talk about it together.

Pee Thoo Lei, who worked in Manerplaw but lived in Pa He Lu, looked after social welfare tasks. Pee Thoo Lei was very good natured, and I sometimes stayed in her house. Her husband, Padoh Baw U Paw, who was a friend of my husband, had two roles, one as a KNDO brigadier and one as a paramilitary officer responsible for policing. She had one son who was a medic in the KNDO and whose wife was president of an orphanage in Kawthoolei, traveling abroad to the countries that supported her work.

Naw Lah Po was a good friend and loved me a lot, so whenever I needed anything, she helped me. She had seven children, three girls and four boys. One of her sons is a battalion commander in the KNLA.

Ku Paw was responsible for the economic and business side, including the shops. She was a lot younger than me, but she died of cancer after we arrived in Australia. Her husband, Pastor Robert, managed the refugee camps on the border, working with the UN.[2]

Shwe Paw was in charge of the office administration in Manerplaw. She was also younger than me. Her husband was a junior army officer, but he was killed in action after Manerplaw fell in the mid-1990s. She is still living in Karen State.

Ka Prey was vice chairwoman and treasurer of the KWO and her husband was the head of the KNU education department.

---

2. During the 2000s, the refugee population in official camps along the Thai border reached around a hundred and fifty thousand persons, mostly Karen but also Karenni and Mon. Since 1984, the aid program has been coordinated by the Thai Burma Border Consortium (TBBC), today known as the Border Consortium, which produces regular reports on the humanitarian situation (Burmese Border Consortium 2004). In addition, there were over two million migrants, both legal and illegal, working in Thailand, many of whom had also fled the conflict in Burma.

There were four levels to the KWO: village, district, province, and general headquarters. The district levels would then go out to the villages. This echoed the KNU system of administration on the Burmese side of the border with Thailand, in which there were seven districts.

I wanted to do the organizer's job because some Karen women didn't have any education, so I wanted to empower them. I liked organizing as I think I am quite well organized.

My duty was to go out each month to the districts and coordinate the KWO and its structure in the townships and villages in the seven Karen districts. In each village I gathered all the women, explained the objective and the work of the KWO, and encouraged them to become members. There would usually be twenty or thirty women of all ages. Whenever I organized meetings in a village, we educated women about their rights under KNU law and any other women's issues. We encouraged women to go to school. Before the meetings, we would give them information sheets and talk with them about women's rights. At the meeting, they would put together the KWO for their village and form the governing structure, which would be filled by elections. We kept a list of all the members on a worksheet. My work as a teacher helped me in my work with the KWO, enabling me to better communicate with the villagers.

Women liked to join the KWO because it looked after them. If the women were on their own and not part of the KWO, the KWO would not know of their difficulties, and they would be suffering by themselves. If they became members of the KWO, the organization watched over them. If anything happened to a woman, she could go to the KWO and settle it. So they felt safer and stronger by coming together and being within the KWO. If they were alone, it was difficult to face problems, but together they could share their problems and work more effectively.

Because the men joined the army or filled other roles in the revolution or went away to find work, the women had to do everything: grow crops, look after children, cook and clean. The women didn't go to other villages so they didn't know how to get and sow seeds. The KWO took responsibility for seed distribution and for teaching each household how to survive.

The KNU and KWO would sometimes go together to villages. We would always check, however, to see if there was fighting in the area before we went to a village. Because of fighting we couldn't go to some provinces, but if the KNU was there we were able to enter the villages.

The Burmese army's eyes were always on the KNU, but the KWO was outside the view of the Burmese eyes, so we could go and organize education in places the KNU could not reach. Even in our own "liberated areas," the KNU was unable to reach some remote territories. So, although it was the responsibility of the KNU to organize education, the women organized out-of-reach schools and coordinated the teachers who would be responsible for each village.

While I was with the KWO I also learned about women's rights, in particular their rights in the home. Before joining the KWO, I thought it was OK for men to hit women as it was part of our tradition. But now I know it is wrong. In traditional Karen culture, men made all the decisions, but I learned that women had the right to make decisions too. When I came to Australia, I realized that women's rights are real and that men and women are equal, with men cooking and looking after children too.

In the KWO, we also talked about women's rights to work and do the same jobs as men, such as office work. The KWO's education department encouraged women to study in their village and pursue further education, like medical studies in Manerplaw.

Women have more power if they are educated. If they don't have education, they don't know about discrimination or about what's happening around them and they can be easily be controlled by men. They may not know that domestic violence is wrong or how to deal with it and so they simply keep silent.

In Karen culture, the man is the head of the household and the wife is second, so the men have more power in the household. There is no divorce in Karen culture, so if they beat us, we couldn't do anything. The village chief would discuss marital problems with a couple only if the situation was really bad, such as when men got drunk and couldn't control themselves.

Before the KWO was formed, when men became angry, they would sometimes beat their wives and children. The KNU had rules and regulations to stop domestic violence, but it still happened. After the KWO branches became active, the men couldn't do this because the KNU could enforce our rules and regulations. The process was as follows: if a man beat his wife, she would go to the KWO. They took responsibility and called the husband to the office to explain that he must not do this. The KWO only gave advice about what to do. If the man didn't listen to their advice and still beat his family, the KWO arranged a safe place for the victim and told the KNU to take action. If the perpetrator was sent to the KNU, he would go to the KNU court. If found guilty at the KNU court, he would face legal consequences. If the case was strong, he could go to jail.

Before this program, domestic violence was a big problem. Husbands would get drunk and do whatever they wanted to their families. After the program, in some provinces where the husbands drank palm wine, the women started to cut down the palm trees because they knew their rights.

Traditionally, women didn't have any opportunities or a voice. By coming together in the KWO, women became empowered, and the men had to deal with the consequences. Not surprisingly, some in the KNLA didn't like the KWO. It was a period of social change for Karens, and the KWO had managed part of that change. I was excited to be part of it.

The KWO ran basic health training, including hygiene, for villagers. They also sent their staff to undertake nursing training or similar studies. When they passed their training, they were sent to remote villages to teach women and advise them on cleanliness, hygiene, pregnancy, and giving birth.

They advised women to go to the hospital to give birth rather than doing so at home where they might risk their lives. When women gave birth in their own homes, two or three children would die out of every ten births. There was a very high infant mortality rate. Babies would go into shock or get infections when umbilical cords were cut because the women didn't know what to do. The KWO also trained midwives for the villages, so if women couldn't go to the hospital, a midwife could assist them.

The main health problems were malaria and diarrhea. The health department officials would go to the districts and invite women to get training in health and maternal health in particular. After their training, they would go back to the villages and be able to dispense some medication like quinine (for malaria) through the KWO. The KWO was particularly concerned with women's health and women's problems. But we didn't talk about contraception because we didn't know about it and it wasn't available. In Christianity, children are blessings from God.

The KWO was concerned with all aspects of a woman's life, including problems of adultery, polygamy, trafficking, and prostitution. If there were soldiers who went to the front line and committed adultery, the KWO helped the wives. The KNU made monogamy the law. If anyone violated the law there could be serious consequences. One of my son's teachers was executed for adultery. If women were raped or had a similar problem they could not settle, they could approach the KNU and it took responsibility and went to court so a jury could decide. In the villages, some women were sexually abused by Burmese soldiers or by other villagers.

The KWO also educated women about trafficking and prostitution. Women were promised jobs in Thailand where they could work and earn money for their families. But when they went there they would find that the promised work was prostitution. A Thai man would come to the displaced persons camp in Burma where they were hiding from the Burmese soldiers and finding it difficult to get enough food. He would tell them that there was lots of work in Thailand, and some women followed him.

Once, twelve women were asked to go to Thailand to work in a house but ended up in prostitution. When the KWO heard the news, they asked the KNU to get the military or the police to stop them. Female soldiers who were also members of the KWO went and rescued all the women. The women were very happy when the KWO discovered them because some had been sold into prostitution and had lost hope because they knew of no way to escape. When women did try to run away on their own the KWO took responsibility for them including providing medical treatment if they had diseases. Not only were the women very happy to be rescued from that way of life; the woman's home village was also happy because they hadn't known how to find her. They were angry with the traffickers and brothel owners who did this to the women.

Nobody dared to try this with me because I was a general's wife, but other women whose husbands were away were vulnerable. The problem is that people would secretly go to Thailand to find work and support their families because life was hard in Burma. When they were attacked and forced into prostitution, they dared not open their mouths to protest because they were afraid. I never went to investigate because I didn't have Thai citizenship. The Thai knew we were KWO, so they would have interfered. We had to send those Karens who lived in Thailand to investigate the trafficking so that the Thai authorities wouldn't notice.

In 1987, the KWO general secretary said she wanted to step down. They asked me to take over. When they asked me to do it, I felt like I had a fever and the whole night I couldn't sleep. I was afraid that I wouldn't be able to understand the secretary's job and that it would be too great a burden for me. But I became the general secretary anyway. Through experience and training I learned how to do the job. Shwe Paw already knew the work of a general secretary from when she was KWO officer and she helped me.

For the annual general meeting, I had to take responsibility for compiling all the reports from the village, township, and district levels. Each village sent their annual report to the township, who sent theirs to the district, and then on to the central level. I had to combine them into one yearly report for the whole organization. At the meeting I had to read this annual report and answer any questions. I loved my job even if it was stressful and I didn't like writing the reports after our trips.

I had to a do a lot of public speaking, which I liked a lot, but I liked the meetings the most as I liked talking to everyone. If the KNU asked us to do something, it was my job to inform the districts and provinces by sending letters. People traveling to the district would take our letters with them as there was no postal system. When the provincial officers had to come to headquarters for one reason or another, they would take letters with them to and from headquarters. It would take about three days to get from headquarters to the districts.

Every four years the KWO had a congress and reorganized. At the congress in 1989, I was elected general secretary of the KWO, the role I had been doing for the past two years. I was reelected as general secretary in 1993. I think they elected me because I was a hard worker.

I also had to take responsibility for finances and do a financial audit. We had thousands of women members as most adult Karen women joined the KWO and paid a membership fee of two Thai baht per person per year. At the time this was the cost of one egg. The membership fees were distributed to the various levels of the organization: the branches would send 10 percent of the membership fees to the district, the district would then send 10 percent to the province, and the province would send 10 percent to headquarters.

We also got money from KWO businesses, such as farming, livestock, and shops. From my memory, the budget per year was just over a hundred thousand Thai baht. The KWO kept shops that used Thai baht. When we opened shops we sometimes had to borrow capital from the KNU, which we paid back out of our profits. After paying back our loan, we kept the profits. Sometimes we would get money from international women's NGOs. Overall we were good at getting money, running businesses, and balancing the accounts.

If we needed money, we would discuss our needs and allocate the money, once the treasurer had approval from the chairperson or secretary. If we didn't have enough money, we could borrow from the KNU. For example, we could use this money to go to the annual general meetings and the congress meetings. The KWO paid as much as they could, but if they were still in need, the KNU would help us. Although the KWO was under the KNU, it had its own work that needed to be financed too. Sometimes we experienced financial hardship when, according to the reports, the accounts were not correct. So, we had to investigate and fix up accounts. I would help mentor the younger women. This is just part of our culture. Some of these women went on to be leaders in the KWO.

All my KWO friends spent time in the office. We lived in different areas, but we all came together at the office in Manerplaw, which was the headquarters for the KNU, KWO, and KNLA. Everyone stayed in Manerplaw from Monday to Friday and went home on the weekends. I lived in Htoo Wah Lu and sometimes I would go home on the weekend, if work wasn't too busy. I went in a pickup truck from Htoo Wah Lu to Manerplaw, which was an easy journey, but sometimes I had to walk, which was not easy.

I would start work at 10 a.m. and finish at about 4 p.m. Sometimes we had to prepare reports, so we would sleep at the office because all the detail took time. I liked going to work every day. My niece, Htoo Htoo's daughter, lived with us and studied in Htoo Wah Lu, so she looked after our animals and helped Paw Nay Thah, who was still in school. Everyone knew each other and we all lived close together.

THE FALL OF MANERPLAW

In the mid-1990s there were conflicts between Buddhist and Christian Karens. I was really scared that there would be a split in Karen society. I had friends who were Buddhist. There had never been any conflict between the Buddhists and Christians in the KWO. The Burmese army tried to influence the Buddhist Karens and persuade the two religious groups to separate so that the Karens would be less powerful. They weren't really trying to influence the women. When U Thuzana and his followers built the temples, they asked the Buddhist women to help build them. If they said no, though, they would force them to build.

When the split happened, I understood that the Karen soldiers in the new Democratic Karen Buddhist Army (DKBA) had to show the Burmese that they were against the KNLA. When they were supporting the Burmese, they were no longer Karen. They were blinded; they didn't see that they were hurting Karens.

This was the first time I had experienced conflict since my children were small. I was upset because for thirty years we had lived peacefully. But because of the split between the two religions, we had conflict again. I was really upset about Karens fighting Karens but there was nothing I could do.

The KNU told the KWO that fighting might start so it was best that all the KWO's documents be moved to a safe place. We took everything to another place in Klaw Taw. We kept going with our work. Then they asked us to leave Manerplaw and go back to our houses.

From the KWO office, we evacuated by boat to Htoo Wah Lu. At Htoo Wah Lu a river divides Burma and Thailand, with Htoo Wah Lu in Thailand.

They had already been fighting for about two or three months, but it hadn't reached Manerplaw yet.

I knew that Ralph was safe because he was in the KNU base at Wangkha to the south. My children were away from the fighting too. Ler Paw lived in the Sixth Brigade area further south from Mae Sot on the border. His wife was heavily pregnant with their first child, Ernest. Like me with Ler Paw, she had to flee to Thailand with Ernest in her stomach. Ler Gay and Paw Nay Thah were in Chiang Mai and Mina was in Australia.

The children of the village were evacuated early to Pway Baw Lu. Some of the KWO ladies lived in Pway Baw Lu on the Thai side. Lah Po was in that village. To begin with they were safe there but later on they all had to leave Pway Baw Lu.

I had stayed in Htoo Wah Lu because the village chief hadn't ordered us to leave yet. He had told the children to leave but not us. About a week later the Burmese army attacked Manerplaw.

At about 9 or 10 p.m. a KNLA officer came to my house while I was praying. Despite the urgency of the situation, he waited for me to finish praying. Then he told me to evacuate. I got some rice, a pot for the rice, and a machete. In the mountains there were small streams where I could get water, but I would need a machete to cut wood to build a fire. I also took a radio, some clothes, a Bible, and a blanket. I had already put everything aside in preparation for leaving. That's why we were ready to evacuate so quickly.

Less than half an hour after the officer came to my house, all the villagers fled together: more than sixty people. We just went away—not anywhere in particular, just away from the fighting. I fled together with my nieces La Ku and Ta Kaw Paw, Ta Kaw Paw's husband Ko Toe, and their first child, who was about eight months old. Ta Kaw Paw carried her baby on her back and clothes on her front. Together we climbed the mountains all night to escape.

If I had taken a torch, the Burmese soldiers would have seen us, so I didn't take one. When we went up the mountains on the Thai side, DKBA soldiers were just on the other side of the river; if we had shone torches, they would still have been able to see us. Instead, we walked by the light of the moon.

The first night, Ko Toe had to go back and get more things after we met up with others because we hadn't been able to carry it all ourselves. We waited in the hills for him to come back with more things. Then we walked until 1 a.m.

We were still within range of bombs and we could hear the gunfire as we left. One of the young ladies with us, who worked for my friend, grabbed her chest and started shaking when she heard the gunfire. At the time we thought it was a heart attack, but now I think it was a panic attack. We didn't know what a panic attack was. Someone carried her. This was probably the first time she had heard gunfire so close.

The whole village couldn't go together, but there was only one road, so we separated. Those at the northern end of Manerplaw went north up the mountains, and those at the southern end went south along the river. We went along a small path up the mountains. It was really hard walking. Sometimes we reached a cliff, or a waterfall and we had to go around it. While I was walking, I wasn't thinking about anything. I was really scared. I was only dreaming that one day I would live a peaceful life.

The DKBA was all along the Moei River on the other side. When we reached the top of the mountain, we could see the fire burning in Manerplaw. We watched it burn and we were totally devastated. But I didn't cry—there were no tears left, I had cried too much before.

We slept for a little while and then continued walking, but DKBA soldiers were shooting at the side of the river we were on, at Htoo Wah Lu. Everyone had left but they were still shooting. The DKBA fired big guns that made very loud "boom" sounds. The KNLA was firing back at the DKBA.

Each morning we cooked, then we would pack up and walk all day, climbing the mountains. We carried rice, chili peppers, and fish paste. When the women were cooking, the men would go and search for prawns or small fish in the streams. There were about ten families in our group.

Two weeks after we left, one of the women gave birth. Fortunately, there was a midwife in the group. One of the old men in our group died from malaria and fever.

We travelled every day except Saturday and Sunday, when we would rest all day. We had a pastor with us, so we had a worship service. The pastor told us that whenever we had worries, we should pray. When we face troubles, we should give our problems to God. I think that's how I've survived until now. I always ask God to give me strength and energy.

When I fled the Japanese, I was too young, I didn't know anything and didn't worry. When I fled from the Burmese, I was really upset and worried all the time. I was really upset this time too because it was Karens fighting Karens. I was so tired, I wasn't well, and we had to climb the mountains. At the time I had malaria. I had been to the villages to do a welfare visit and I got a cold or flu and, after that, asthma. Then I got malaria. I found it hard to run. At the time I was sixty-two years old, so it was even harder.

We eventually reached a Thai Karen village, in the farm area of Kaw Lar Wa Paw, where about thirty or forty people lived. Kaw Lar Wa Plaw means "English field." There's a building there to remember the English missionaries, and the Roman Catholics had built a church.

The United Nations had heard about the fighting and they knew people were fleeing, so they had set up tents with food. I felt safer there. We were very lucky because they had food, and we had eaten almost all our food. We stayed a few days, then the UNHCR helped us get to Mae Ra Moh, a new refugee camp.

Mae Ra Moh camp was built on a river called Mae Ra Moh. People were on both sides of the river. We left Kaw Lar Wa at 4 p.m. and reached Mae Ra Moh at nighttime. We were some of the first to arrive.

We didn't have tents when we reached Mae Ra Moh. It was night and dark, so we slept on mats. The place where we slept was nice and soft. We got a good night's sleep but when we woke up we discovered we had been sleeping on elephant dung!

We knew that we would have to stay at Mae Ra Moh so we needed to build a house. There were no toilets there. Some people had been using the river as a toilet, so it smelled, and it was too crowded by the river. So we built a house a bit higher up the mountain and away from the river. There was a small stream nearby. I lived with Ta Kaw Paw, her husband Ko Toe, and their baby son.

When I evacuated, I left everything behind. Although I was sad about leaving things behind, all the villagers are in the same situation, so you cannot dwell in your sadness. When we left our homes, we left them for good. We never went back. Close to one thousand people lived in Htoo Wah Lu. All of them left. Everyone was in shock; they had had everything in Htoo Wah Lu but they had to leave it all behind. They had a hospital with X-ray machines and so on, but we had to leave everything behind. Some people owned big shops and had to leave everything.

In Mae Ra Moh, I registered with the International Organization of Migration (IOM). We stayed at in the camp for one or two months, then the DKBA attacked the camp even though it was a refugee settlement for those fleeing the conflict in Thailand. The DKBA soldiers came quickly, at around 10 or 11 a.m. They came to our section of the camp (section 1), fired guns, killed some people, and captured others. They burned the houses as they attacked. At the same time the Thai soldiers were trying to defend us with their helicopters. We didn't have any warning; we just had to run. As we ran, we saw people being shot. Many people had blood on them, and I was really scared. My legs froze and I couldn't run.

All I had was a machete in my hand. I was using it when they attacked so I ran with it. Everything else was left behind. I couldn't see the DKBA soldiers; I just heard the gunfire and the screams.

The DKBA left quickly. When we returned to the village, we had to work out who was missing. I knew one of the missing men, Dr. Marta, who was captured. He was a doctor who cared for us at the hospital in Htoo Wah Lu when we were sick. The DKBA knew him and knew he was a doctor. They eventually released him.

I knew some of the DKBA soldiers. It was a betrayal when the DKBA left the KNLA and supported the Burmese. The villagers didn't understand the political situation, so when the Burmese tried to influence them, they easily believed what they said.

Before the conflict started, the KNLA leaders tried to compromise and negotiate, but there was no way to negotiate anymore. After the conflict started, even though they were Karen, the soldiers of the DBKA became the enemy because they started shooting Karen people.

There were some Buddhists who stayed with the KNLA. We weren't angry at the DKBA soldiers; we were angry with the Burmans because, without their plan, nobody would have known how to do so much harm to the Karens. The DKBA was manipulated by the Burmans.

Some houses in the camp burned, but luckily ours didn't because they only burnt the houses by the river. We were higher up, not by the riverside. The other refugees came back and rebuilt.

When Ler Paw's son Ernest was one week old I went to visit them in Bae Klaw camp where they were living. His wife Karen had given birth in a clinic in Mae Sot in Thailand. It was so nice to see my grandson.

One month after the DKBA attacked, I sent Ralph a message and asked him to take me to Palu. I was too scared to stay in Mae Ra Moh anymore. Ralph was around the Sixth Brigade area with Bo Mya. Ralph came by himself to pick me up. He took me to Palu, then he went somewhere else with Bo Mya.

I was so happy to see him again. He was happy that I was leaving Mae Ra Moh because he thought the situation there might get worse. He was scared that I wouldn't be safe there because I was married to a KNLA general and I was part of the KWO.

In Palu I lived on the Thai side of the border. Some of the Karen leaders had houses there so I had somewhere to live. Saw Ler Paw was now in Mae La Camp (Mae La is the name of the Thai village; Bae Klaw is the Karen name for the same place).

At the beginning I had evacuated with La Ku, one of my nieces who had been living with me in Htoo Wah Lu. We remained together, and she came with me to Palu. The DKBA never attacked Palu. But I didn't know how to restart my life and settle there.

Lah Po was living in Mae Sot and she asked me to come to Mae La refugee camp. Saw Ler Paw's wife's family was also moving to Mae La. So, after one month, La Ku and I left Palu and moved to Mae La. We went there by "line car," which was like a pick-up truck. Mae La was a meeting point. It would be convenient for me to find my husband and for him to find me there. My niece Maureen also came to visit me.

When I was at Mae La Camp I opened a shop to earn money. I sold food, betel nut leaf, tobacco, and fish. My customers were the people in the camp. There were lots of people there and they liked betel nut and tobacco, so I was able to sell a lot.

When I opened the shop, I didn't have any money. I asked the KWO for twenty thousand baht, saying that after four months I would repay it all. Once I got the money, I went to Mae Sot to get stock. I was really happy because after I sold things, I could have whatever I wanted to eat. I was independent.

I liked my shop and I was good at business, but I thought the work of the KWO was more important. I always sold everything I bought in Mae Sot. Sometimes I exchanged products for leaves for the roof. We wove them with bamboo to build a house.

After one year, I decided to go back to my KWO work. I handed over my shop to my niece La Ku. First I went to Mae Sot to meet Lah Po. Then I went with Lah Po to Hti Ka Pler village, which was at the border but within Burma. Hti Ka Pler wasn't safe but it was where the KNU were setting up their new headquarters, so they were setting up the KWO there as well. They were starting to build an office there.

The KWO paperwork that had gone to Klaw Taw for safekeeping was then moved to Hti Ka Pler because they were close by. I was happy to start work again. We began work as soon as we built our office. We called back Shwe Paw to come and work in Hti Ka Pler with us. So, it was the three of us. Other women from the Sixth Brigade area joined us. In the KWO we shared the tasks and when we had meetings, some of the committee members joined us.

Only a few leaders and not too many people stayed: just the KNU and KNLA families. It was a small village, smaller than Manerplaw. About twelve or thirteen people worked and lived at the office at Hti Ka Pler. I lived at the KWO department with the other staff and office workers. Lah Po lived in a house with Bo Mya. The women weren't always in the office. They rotated shifts and came and went. We also had barracks. There were some barracks for the women and some for the men. It was like a big family. There were young and old women.

Every time we went fishing, we would go together. We had the KWO shop, so when we needed to buy stock, we would go together, sometimes with the soldiers. We shared the cooking. We ate everything: fish, yellow beans, small crabs from the river, and different types of vegetables from the forest. We also grew our own vegetables and raised animals. There was no guard for the animals, so they could wander anywhere in Hti Ka Pler.

Ralph didn't come to Hti Ka Pler. I only saw him once in the three years I lived there, when I went to get stock in Kyaik Don in Burma. I missed him every day and every night, but I was used to us being apart. We encouraged each other. If we could help the Karens, then this was our duty. We were both doing our duty.

I was happy because we could start growing KWO produce and do our jobs again around the Sixth Brigade area. Also, we could organize training in typewriting for the women. I don't know how to use a typewriter, but others did and they trained the women. We were able to continue our work, and it was quite a peaceful time.

When we rebuilt the KWO, we already had some office equipment but we didn't have a typewriter. So we requested that my niece Maureen send us the money for two typewriters so we could have a second typewriter for training.

Eventually, the Burmese military attacked Hti Ka Pler. One week before the Burmese army attacked, we received warning they would come, so we were prepared to run. We packed up all the KWO stuff and hid important documents with Thai villagers. We took the typewriters and moved our shop to a Thai village. We moved goods by elephants and some by car. A few KWO staff, soldiers, and villagers helped us. We moved everything over the week. We left the day before the Burmese army attacked. This time I left by car. We went to Thailand, to Noe Hpa Doh village.

We were more organized this time than when Manerplaw fell because we received word earlier so we had more time to prepare. Because Bo Mya was in Hti Ka Pler, all the news would come to him, which meant we knew everything sooner.

I was frustrated and angry that we had to move and reorganize everything again. We stayed at Noe Hpa Doe for one night and then went to Noe Po where the UNHCR had set up a camp. Some of the KNU leaders stayed at Noe Hpa Doe. It was safe. Lah Po went to a different place with Bo Mya, and I stayed in Noe Po with the other KWO staff.

I sent a message through the signals department to my husband. I didn't know where he was, but the operators could contact him. I was worried about him with the fighting in the KNLA Sixth Brigade area but he was fine.

After one month I decided to leave Noe Po and the KWO and go back to Mae La where Saw Ler Paw was living with his family. I didn't want to stop working at the KWO, but I wanted to find my children and be with my family. I handed everything to Shwe Paw, the KWO officer. It was a really hard decision to make because I knew Lah Po would be really upset and her eyes would fill with tears. I didn't know if I would be leaving the KWO permanently but I couldn't stay there anymore.

I thought I might return to the KWO but I wanted to see my family. I felt pity for Paw Nay Thah because her leg was not good. I needed to gather all the children together. I didn't leave earlier because I felt I hadn't finished my duty. Now, after we had to move again, I felt it was the right time to go.

It wasn't easy for me to go alone to Mae La because I didn't have any documents. Saw Ler Paw organized for someone from Thai intelligence to come with him to pick me up. Otherwise I would have been arrested in Thailand.

It was 1997 and I was sixty-four years old. I didn't want to retire. I wasn't tired. I wasn't ready. Sometimes I felt it was too complicated and there were too many problems, then I would feel tired. When I went back to Mae La Camp I was worried and scared of DKBA attacks and I couldn't sleep properly.

I asked Ralph and Paw Nay Thah to come to Mae La refugee camp. Ralph came to Noe Po and a Thai intelligence officer and Ler Paw took him to Mae La. Ler Gay stayed in Chiang Mai. I was happy to be living again with my family, but I felt sad for the KWO and especially for Naw Lah Po, because we had worked closely together. She was really happy with my work so she was sad when I left. So, I was happy for my own family but sad for my KWO family—but I could not avoid it.

Mina had gone to Australia in 1994 and I hadn't seen her for a while. She came to visit Mae La camp in 1997. Mina was working in Bangkok teaching English to children. She couldn't come for long and only stayed three days. She encouraged us to come to Australia and advised us to apply to the UN and become refugees. She was worried about us. Mina helped other people in Mae La to apply to come to Australia too. After Mina visited we started talking with the family about going to Australia. Ralph also contacted his brother Howard in Australia.

Life had become too risky because of enemy activities, especially those of the DKBA because they knew all the ins and outs. We couldn't sleep in our own house each night; we had to sleep somewhere else because the DKBA could raid the houses at night. So we could only stay at our house in the daytime. The other problem was that all the locals were Karens. We couldn't differentiate between our Karens and the Burmese Karens. We couldn't trust anyone in the night. That's why Mina, when she came and saw the situation, said that we'd better apply for refugee status.

Ralph and I went together from Mae La to Bangkok where Mina was waiting. Mina had given us the money to go to Bangkok, where she worked to support us. When we got UN support, she gave us the money she had earned and went back to Australia. Maureen came and visited us once and she also gave us some money.

Bo Mya asked Ralph and me to come back. Naw Lah Po had cried when we left for Bangkok. He said he would pay for our travel expenses. When they asked me to come back, I said I wouldn't go. I just told them we wanted to move forward, not back. I never thought I would leave the KWO, so I never officially retired. Ralph had been granted long leave, and I followed him.

Mina and Howard didn't tell us anything about Australia; they just encouraged us to come to this country because it would be good for us—and it would be safe. The situation had been tough and unsafe for us in Thailand, especially for high-ranking officials. Another general had been shot dead in a refugee camp, and General Taru and the district chairman were captured by the DKBA and taken back across the border.

The DKBA weren't targeting Saw Ler Paw or Paw Nay Thah. Saw Ler Paw had lots of friends around the area, so he could escape if necessary. They were safer than us. Ler Paw stayed in Mae La and Paw Nay Thah went back to Chiang Mai where Saw Ler Gay was living. My nieces were younger than my children. La Ku was about seventeen at that time. She wasn't married and she came to Bangkok with us.

We lived in a condominium high up on the fifth floor in the Maneeloy Burmese Student Center near Bangkok. I was very proud of myself. I had only ever lived on the ground level in the forest. I liked living on the fifth floor, but it was very hot. We didn't have a lift, so we had to walk up the stairs. The only problem we had was always being afraid of the Thai police. We had to dress like Thai women: we wore pants, not *longyis*. I cut my hair short. Before I had long hair and I didn't really like it short, but it was for my safety.

I remembered when I slept on elephant poo; now I had a proper mattress. Nothing about Bangkok bothered me: not the cars, not the traffic, nothing. But sometimes I would miss my animals and my house in Htoo Wah Lu.

We couldn't leave the condominium, so we watched a lot of TV. I spent whole days and nights watching Thai TV. I liked the soccer very much and could watch it all night. Ralph was sometimes angry with me. "Soccer has no relevance to you!" he would say. "You have no relatives who play soccer, so why do you spend your whole time watching it on TV?" I liked watching it and I could understand a little Thai.

AUSTRALIA

When we found out we were coming to Australia, I praised God. I made a little feast, invited everyone, and had a thanksgiving service. Before coming to Australia, we went to a training session about Australia in Bangkok. We learned about life in Australia. For example, if the family stays at home rather than eating out, they can save money. I learned about the different colors of cabbage in Australia. We only had one color in Burma. We learned that when we arrived in Australia, we would have to go to Centrelink, the welfare department. I wasn't afraid about going to Australia; I really wanted to go.

On June 1, 2001, we arrived in Perth. We left everything behind us and had a fresh start. From then onwards we had freedom.

The most important thing I wanted to achieve in Australia was to become fluent in English. I really wanted to study it because everyone in Australia speaks English and I wanted to be able to communicate with other people. If I could speak very well, I could talk with my neighbors and tell them about the Bible. I couldn't do anything without learning English.

I studied every day at a vocational collage in Perth. I was so excited and happy to study again. When we arrived at the Perth train station to go to language school, we were so happy because we would meet our classmates and speak in English. My classmates weren't Karens, so we had to speak in English. Some of them spoke English worse than I did, which made me feel better.

But I found that although I learned English in class, by the time I got home, I had forgotten how to speak it. I liked English but there are so many grammar rules; I can't put the words in the right places. One grammar or spelling mistake and the sentence has another meaning.

I was almost seventy years old by the time I arrived in Australia so I was eligible for an old age pension. I looked for a job for a while, but nobody wanted me to work for them. I wanted to learn to drive but I was too old to learn.

In Australia, everything was different from Thailand and Burma. For example, there are toilets everywhere: in train stations and in shopping centers. Everything here is clean.

Now I understand a lot of English compared to when we arrived. I am able to get by. I can catch public transport and do grocery shopping. I'm resourceful like that. I think my resourcefulness comes from my childhood. I can do better here than in Burma. In Burma, we didn't have a doctor or hospital, so when someone was sick, it was really hard, and we had to use traditional medicine. Here in Australia when we feel sick we just go to the doctor or hospital.

I had prayed for years for Ralph to stop drinking and never stopped praying for that. After we came to Perth he stopped drinking, and I felt like a heavy load had been lifted and felt more confident when we went places.

I feel happy with Ralph now. He was born again and has changed in a positive way. Before I worried for him so much: for his safety and his eternal life. My relationship with Ralph is easier now and I don't need to look after him as a small child. Now we have become a happy couple.

Before we didn't have the chance to live together because he had responsibilities and I had responsibilities. Now, wherever we go, we go together. We always sit together. We know each other and are closer because we spend all our time together.

I tell young couples who are about to get married that they will face difficulties building a new life, so they need to be patient, understand each other, and be considerate of each other.

From when I was a small child and the Japanese invaded to when we came to Australia, life has been hard. I depended on God through it all and he has always been with me. This gave me comfort, strength, and encouragement. I felt God intervened and saved us many times when the situation was hopeless. Sometimes when I lie down in bed before I go to sleep, I think about everything that has happened to me. I nearly died, but everything is OK because I have my faith.

We count our blessings every year. On the first anniversary of the day we arrived in Australia, we celebrated and thanked God with a prayer service. From then on other Karen refugees in Perth have started to do the same thing. There are so many prayer services and they want to have it on the anniversary of their arrival.

After we came to Australia we stopped talking about the war. I wanted to clear everything from my mind and not recall the past.

Even though Australia is a peaceful country, when I first arrived I was really afraid of the police. In Thailand we were always afraid that the police would arrest us and send us back to the Burmese side of the border.[1]

When I met a policeman in Australia I was very scared. But here the police don't bother you. In fact, they help you if you are in trouble. Once, a few months after we arrived, I was going home from English class on the train and fell asleep. I went right to the end of the line on the train and woke up in Armadale, on the outskirts of Perth. I went up to the transit police and one officer asked if I was ok. I told them that I had fallen asleep and asked them where to go. They asked where I wanted to go. I said Gosnells and they showed me the way. "Use the same train back and get off at Gosnells." "I don't know where my house is," I said. So, they drove me back to Gosnells and didn't ask for any money. I like living in Australia because we don't have to be scared.

When we arrived, we all lived in the same house with my children and grandchildren. Then they all moved out. Mina was married in Perth after we came to Australia. She lives in Brisbane, on the other side of the country, with her Australian husband, Jason. When I miss her, I just call. I talk to her almost every day.

I still do the cooking and the cleaning. I have done housework and chores for seventy years. That was how I got strong arms. I used to like housework but now I'm fed up with it. I don't want to do it anymore but there is no one else to do it for us. In Kawthoolei, if anyone needed help you could go and help them. But here everyone has their own work to do, so they are too busy to help each other. When we need things, we go to the shops ourselves. My children are busy, so Ralph and I look mostly after ourselves.

I have eight grandchildren. The refugee youth in Australia have to study at a high level. It's vastly different from the olden days when I was a child in Burma. They learn English well, so they don't need interpreters.

I am often with one of my youngest grandchildren, Julia. When I was small I was like my granddaughter Julia: very outgoing. I was confident in speaking and singing, talking with other people. I always acted in plays at school. Julia never says no when asked to do something. She likes to be around people.

---

1. Refugees in Thailand are confined to the designated refugee camps; the Thai authorities consider those found outside the camps to be illegal immigrants. Thus, if found outside of the camps, the refugees are often arrested and can be deported back to Burma. The documents provided by the UNHCR hardly protect the refugees when confronted by the police. As a result, Burmese refugees often come to develop an immense fear of the police. Burmese refugees in Malaysia also report a similar experience.

For fun, I like to go fishing. My favorite thing to cook is fish because I used to have fish in my village. So, when I cook fish it brings back happy memories. I still go fishing with my son. We drive up to Jurien Bay, a seaside town two hours north of Perth.

We are very busy now. We go to church and attend many Bible studies and prayer meetings. We go to a multicultural seniors' group once a week where I have made lots of friends. We travel to other parts of Australia like Brisbane to visit Mina and Sydney and Melbourne to visit other friends and relatives.

Since coming to Perth I have made new friends, mostly Karens. All are younger than me. People my age here can't walk because they are tired. So they stay home and people visit them.

I have made friends through the church here. I used to teach Sunday school at our church in Perth. The only thing I still want to do here is missionary work. I want to tell more people about God. I visited Brisbane, Melbourne, Sydney, and Thailand to do missionary work. Through my testimony, I hope people will get more energy. Whenever people face challenges, I hope they will remember my testimony.

It can be difficult for refugees to settle in Australia. Some have struggled to find jobs. But I think it was a good decision for us to come to Australia because life is easier here. The government looks after us with old age pensions and we have a house. Whatever we want to eat, we can eat.

We don't have to worry, and we can give some money away. Sometimes we can donate money back to Thailand and Burma to help relatives and others. It's important to me that we send money back because the scripture says you need to love your neighbor and help your neighbor. When you help your neighbor, you feel happier and not guilty.

When you help others, they help you also. Sometimes I bring food to my neighbor in Gosnells and sometimes they bring food to us. We have a good relationship. When we first arrived, our neighbors were aboriginal Australians. We got on really well with them. When their children saw me, they would come and give me a big hug. When they moved away, they left a letter in our mailbox saying we were good neighbors.

Now we are in Gosnells and we feel at home, but I still prefer my house in Htoo Wah Lu. There were streams there where we could get water all day and night. We could go down and take a bath in the stream. With bamboo pipes, the water could go directly into the house, so we could bathe in the stream or in the house.

The garden had fruit and vegetables for each season. We planted many pineapple, mango, orange, and banana trees. The water came through to the garden and drained away. We were able to raise some fish to eat. When I came home from the office, I didn't go in to the house. I'd always go to look at the fish in the pond first. I would like to go back to Htoo Wah Lu and visit, but it's all jungle now.

I don't really communicate with the KWO anymore. All the KWO women I worked with have retired. Lah Po and Pee Thoo Lei are still in Thailand. Sometimes we talk on the phone and I see them when I visit Thailand. We all go and eat in a particular restaurant. When we talk we feel so happy but sad that we don't live together. We were like sisters and I miss them.

Both Pee Thoo Lei's and Naw Lah Po's husbands have since died. When I visited them in Thailand, I felt pity for them because they are so skinny and tired. They now have many health problems like high blood pressure and diabetes. I don't have any diseases, but I have high blood pressure.

There's a new generation running the KWO now and I don't know any of them. They don't have difficulties with their age. The minds of the youth are very sharp and they can raise money from many sources. They go to NGOs directly rather than waiting for NGOs to come to Karen State. The NGOs go to them at the village level, bringing food and clothing. In our time we couldn't afford to do this.

The standard of their work is very high. There are some foreigners who go to the KWO office and teach them about office work: how to run the KWO and organize training for villagers. When I visited, I saw foreigners teaching. In our time, we couldn't speak English. We needed interpreters when foreigners came to communicate with us. Now the youth all speak English and many have studied in England and America, so their standard is higher than in our time.

FIGURE 12.   Sheera with a kangaroo, Perth

My brother Ten Boy still lives in Burma, in Yay Aye Kyun, an island below Tavoy in Burma's far south. He moved there because when the KNLA went to his former village they kept him as a village elder and whenever they needed advice, they asked him. When the Burmese soldiers came, they also went to him. When the Burmese army came, they heard that the KNLA was also going to him, so he was stuck between the two sides. The Burmese tortured him and hurt his head. After the Burmese soldiers left, he went south so he wouldn't need to deal with the Burmans or the Karens again. The Burmans there didn't know him or why he came there. They keep him as their headman. He is an elder now. It is peaceful there and he says he won't move anymore.

They don't have the Internet where he lives, so I can't speak to him. I saw him and some other relatives for three days in Thailand in 2014. I was so happy to see him, and we talked constantly. They were all so skinny. I gave them everything I came with and I went home without my suitcase.

I want the Karens to have Kawthoolei, their own state, and freedom: freedom of speech, freedom of everything. When I travel in Thailand I have an Australian passport but I always say I am Karen. I am Karen first and Australian second.

I want to visit Burma, but I don't want to live there. I want to visit the village I was born in and I want to do missionary work in Kawthoolei. In Perth, sometimes we go to the beach at sunset and I miss my Et Et village.

References

Amnesty International. 1999. "The Kayin (Karen) State: Militarization and Human Rights." AI Index: 16/12/99.

Amnesty International. 2019. "'No One Can Protect Us': War Crimes and Abuses in Myanmar's Rakhine State." AI Index: ASA 16/0417/2019

Aung-Thwin, Michael, and Maitrii Aung-Thwin. 2012. *A History of Myanmar Since Ancient Times: Traditions and Transformations*. London: Reaktion Books.

Burmese Border Consortium. 2004. *Twenty Years on the Border*. Bangkok: Burmese Border Consortium.

Callahan, Mary P. 2003. *Making Enemies: War and State Building in Burma*. Ithaca, NY: Cornell University Press.

Cheesman, Nick. 2003 "School, State and Sangha in Burma." *Comparative Education* 39: 45–63.

Chin, Ko-Lin. 2016. *The Golden Triangle: Inside Southeast Asia's Drug Trade*. Ithaca, NY: Cornell University Press.

Craig, Charmaine. 2017. *Miss Burma*. New York: Grove Press.

Dun, Smith. 1980. *Memoirs of the Four-Foot Colonel*. Ithaca: Cornell Southeast Asia Program.

Falla, Jonathan. 1991. *True Love and Bartholomew: Rebels on the Burmese Border*. Cambridge: Cambridge University Press.

Gibson Richard M., with Wenhua Chen. 2011. *The Secret Army*. Singapore: John Wiley & Sons.

Gravers, Mikael. 2001. "Cosmology, Prophets, and Rebellion among the Buddhist Karen in Burma and Thailand." *Moussons: Recherche en sciences humaines sur l'Asie du Sud-Est* 4: 3–31.

Gravers, Mikael. 2015. "Disorder as Order: The Ethno-Nationalist Struggle of the Karen in Burma/Myanmar—A Discussion of the Dynamics of an Ethnicized Civil War and Its Historical Roots." *The Journal of Burma Studies* 19: 27–78.

Gravers, Mikael. 2018. "A Saint in Command? Spiritual Protection, Justice, and Religious Tensions in the Karen State." *Independent Journal of Burmese Research* 2: 87–119.

Karen Human Rights Group. 2008. *Village Agency: Rural Rights and Resistance in a Militarized Karen State*. KHRG no. 2008-03. Available online at http://khrg.org/sites/default/files/khrg0803.pdf

Keyes, Charles, ed. 1979. *Ethnic Adaptation and Identity: The Karen on the Thai Frontier with Burma*. Philadelphia: Institute for the Study of Human Issues.

Kramer, Tom, Oliver Russell, and Martin Smith. 2018. *From War to Peace in Kayah (Karenni) State: A Land at the Crossroads in Myanmar*. Amsterdam: Transnational Institute.

Kratoska, Paul H. 2002. "The Karen of Burma under Japanese Rule." In *Southeast Asian Minorities in the Wartime Japanese Empire*, edited by Paul H. Kratoska, 21–38. Abingdon: RoutledgeCurzon.

Lehman, F. K. (Kris). 1967. "Burma: Kayah Society as a Function of the Shan-Burman-Karen Context." In *Contemporary Change in Traditional Societies*, edited by Julian Haynes Steward, 1–104. Urbana: University of Illinois Press.

Marshall, Harry I. 1922. *The Karen People of Burma: A Study in Anthropology and Ethnology*. Columbus: University of Columbus, Ohio State.

Morrison, Ian. 1947. *Grandfather Longlegs: The Life and Gallant Death of Maj. H. P. Seagrim*. London: Faber and Faber.

Phan, Zoya, with Damien Lewis. 2009. *Little Daughter: A Memoir of Survival in Burma and the West*. London: Simon and Schuster.

Po, San C. 1928. *Burma and the Karens*. London: Elliot Stock.

Rogers, Benedict. 2004. *A Land Without Evil*. Oxford: Monarch Books.

Selth, Andrew. 2002. *Burma's Armed Forces: Power Without Glory*. Norwalk, CT: Eastbridge Books.

Smeaton, Donald M. 1887. *The Loyal Karens of Burma*. London: Kegan Paul, Trench & Co.

Smith, Martin T. 1991. *Burma: Insurgency and the Politics of Ethnicity*. London: Zed Books. 2nd ed., 1999.

South, Ashley. 2011. *Burma's Longest War: Anatomy of the Karen Conflict*. Amsterdam: Transnational Institute.

Steinberg, David I., and Hongwei Fan. 2012. *Modern China-Myanmar Relations: Dilemmas of Mutual Dependence*. Copenhagen: NIAS Press.

Thawnghmung, Ardeth M. 2008. *The Karen Revolution in Burma: Diverse Voices, Uncertain End*. Policy Studies 45. Washington, DC: East-West Center.

Thawnghmung, Ardeth M. 2012. *The "Other" Karen in Myanmar: Ethnic Minorities and the Struggle Without Arms*. Lanham, MD: Lexington Books.

Turnell, Sean. 2009. *Fiery Dragons: Banks, Moneylenders and Microfinance in Burma*. Copenhagen: NIAS Press.

United National Human Rights Council (UNHRC). 2018. *Report of the Independent International Fact-Finding Mission on Myanmar*. A/HRC/39/64. Advance Unedited Version.

Index

Aaron, Major, 74*f*, 83
adultery, 146
Ah Pu (Claris), 60–61
alcohol, 82, 107, 124–25
Alexander, Charlie, 48
All Burma Students Democratic Front
(ABSDF), 90
American Baptist Mission School (ABM
School), 17–18, 19
annas, 51
Anti-Fascist Organization (AFO), 29
Anti-Fascist People's Freedom League
(AFPFL), 30
artillery, 35–36, 38–39, 54–55
Aung Din, 60
Aung San Suu Kyi, 8, 21, 26n7, 29, 111
Aung-Thwin, Maureen, 87, 153, 156
Australia
Ralph and Sheera arrive in, 104, 158
Ralph and Sheera begin process to go to,
102, 156
Ralph and Sheera settle in, 106–7, 158–63
refugees in, 109–10, 159, 160, 161

Ba Chit, 70, 71
Bala Sein, 54
bamboo
cooking with, 45
cutting, 75
used as pipes, 161
Bangkok, 65, 87–88, 101, 102–3, 156–57
Ba Thin, 44, 98
Ba Tin, 115, 120, 122, 131
Battle of Insein, 2, 3–4, 32–43, 46, 104–5, 121
Ba U Gyi, 3, 33, 36, 42, 55–56
Baw Baw, 125–26
Baw Yu Paw, 85, 86–87, 143
Benson, Louisa, 67
Bewy Paw, 116
Bible school, 123–25
Billy, Major, 54
black market, 83
body lice, 119
Bo Mya

demotes Major Aaron, 83
and fall of Manerplaw, 95, 98
and forcible recruitment into KNLA, 93,
94–95
in Hti Ka Pler, 154, 155
as hunter, 81–82
as leader, 5, 64, 66–67, 76
operations planning and, 79
on Ralph's drinking, 82
and Ralph's retirement, 103–4, 156
Bond, Allan, 52
Border Guard Force (BGF), 7. *See also*
Democratic Karen Buddhist Army
(DKBA)
Bo San Gyaw, 54
Bo San Kyi, 133
Bo Win, 56
British and British rule, 20, 27–28, 29–31,
118, 121
Buddhist Karens, 4n3, 94–97, 149–57
buffalo, 22–23
Burma
under British rule, 20, 118, 121
contemporary, 10*map*
following Japanese occupation, 29–31
future of, 8
harassment of Karens in, 120–22
independence of, 121
Japanese occupation of, 2, 21–31, 118–19
Karen population in, 4n3
news from, 110
during Ralph and Sheera's times, 9*map*
Ralph on current situation in, 110–11
refugees visit, 110
Burma Defence Army (BDA), 26n7
Burma Independence Army (BIA), 21
Burma Locomotive Railway Workshop, 31, 32
Burma National Army (BNA), 26
Burmese army
attacks Hti Ka Pler, 155
captures Sheera, 134–36
tactics of, 56–57, 61, 68, 77–78, 133–34
Burmese Territorial Forces, 32
Burmese Way to Socialism, 5, 6, 64, 68, 89–90

CPSIA information can be obtained
at www.ICGtesting.com
Printed in the USA
LVHW091258020120
642338LV00002B/293/P